I0482922

Leveraging Celebrity Power for Branding

Kisholoy Roy

All rights reserved. No part of this book may be reproduced by any means whatsoever, either electronic or mechanical; including photocopying, recording, or by any information storage and retrieval system, without permission in writing from the aforementioned copyright holder.

Published by
Kisholoy Roy

To my parents

**for their invaluable love and support
and the unconditional sacrifices made.**

About the Book

Andy Warhol, the noted American artist and filmmaker had once predicted, "The day will come when everyone will be famous for 15 minutes." Our present times probably reflect the basic essence of his thoughts as there is an entire generation in today's society that is striving every moment to seek fame and adulation. Surveys among today's youth have revealed that they aspire to become famous above anything else. Probably they have strong gut feeling that being a celebrity or a kind of semi-celebrity is the only avenue for some one to sustain and get noticed in today's world.
True, as per the recent trends, it pays to become famous and hence each and very conscious step taken in turning oneself into a durable celebrity brand yields rich dividends.

This book presents various instances through its chapters where marketers have been found to leverage the selling and convincing power of celebrities in making brands more appealing and salable. The book talks of the science behind endorsements and also how various marketers in the Indian context have ensured optimal utilization of celeb power in marketing their brands across product categories. The book also offers two dissertation works that were done under the guidance of the author by his students. has two major sections.

This book should be of interest to students, researchers as well as professionals.

Contents

Brand Endorsement: Leveraging Celebrity Power

Sourav Ganguly and the Interesting Case of Brand Endorsements

Fragrances and Celebrities: Understanding the Correlation

The Making of 'Youth' Brands

Celebrity Endorsements: How They Shaped Brand Bikini's Identity?

Brand Lux and Movie Stars: The Cinematic Connection

Dissertation – I : Celebrity Endorsements On Television And Its Impact On Brands

Dissertation – II: Analyzing The Impact Of Celebrity Endorsements: Goods V/S Services

Brand Endorsement: Leveraging Celebrity Power

Brand endorsements have been on the rise for quite sometime as far as product/service advertising is concerned. The reason being every brand today wants to be identified with a familiar face and it can only be the celebrities who can fulfil the requirement. As a matter of fact, celebrity endorsements on television have grown six times volume wise between 2003 and 2007 (Exhibit-I). Probing deeper, we find that film personalities have claimed the lion's share when it comes to celebrity endorsements on television. They accounted for 81% of the total endorsements on TV in 2007, of which actors accounted for 50% and actresses accounted for 31%. Sports personalities accounted for 14% of the overall endorsements on television. Hence, it will be politically correct to say that when it comes to brand endorsements, film and sports personalities are the most desirable as brand ambassadors by the ad fraternity.

Exhibit-I
Brand Endorsements: The Growth Index

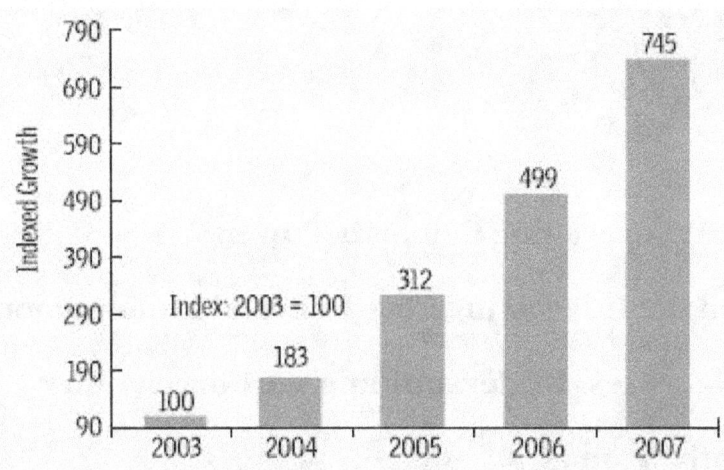

Source: http://www.thehindubusinessline.com

We consider any product/service and we are sure to find a celebrity endorsing it. Either it's a movie personality or a sports icon or a television star. From soft drinks to cars, from watches to shampoos, from banking service to insurance, from public service campaigns to personal computers, celebrities are found making every attempt at invading our perceptual territories. There is a well defined push and pull mechanism that is in operation when it comes to celebrity endorsements as on one hand, celebrities are found to push brand(s) aggressively and on the other hand pull a few millions in their kitty. However, there are a few questions that need to be correctly understood and answered in the context of brand endorsements. First of all, what goes into the making of a successful brand ambassador? Secondly, what decides the duration of a celebrity's selling capacity? Thirdly, what are the factors that decide the market worth of a celebrity in terms of money? Finally, what is the reason behind only a select few celebrities endorsing scores of brands while there are many more celebrities who are not offered endorsement opportunities?

Apart from the performances in their professional domains, there is something called celebrity appeal which earns them endorsement contracts. Celebrities need to project a certain image which should be both identifiable and acceptable to a large consumer segment. Their personality and values should be a reflection of a particular demography in the society. In this context, we can safely cite the example of PepsiCo that has constantly gone for such celebrities who have reflected the tastes, temperaments and attitudes of the emerging Indian youth. Celebrities need to project a consistent image in order to establish themselves as successful brand ambassadors. SRK's 'metrosexual' image, Akshay Kumar's 'dare devil' image, Aishwarya's 'beauty with brain' image, Sachin's 'cool and flamboyant' image, Sourav's 'fighter' image are some examples to be cited. While maintaining a neutral stand in this context, Hari Krishnan, vice-president client servicing at JWT opined, "Celebrities bring a certain image to the table, but ultimately the consumer uses his brain- or his heart! For example, people look up to Akshay Kumar as a macho young man and the imagery fits the bill as far as Thums Up is concerned. Saif has a cool image and it works for the brands he lends his face to." Film actor, Irrfan Khan has a 'thinking guy' image and this has enabled him to establish a symbiotic relationship with Vodafone as the brand ambassador for its operations in India. M.S. Dhoni, the present Indian skipper of the Indian one-day squad has been one cricketer who has witnessed a meteoric rise in his endorsement graph and there have been quite a few factors working in his favour image wise. Judhajit Dutta of Kolkata-based Gameplan Sports (the company managing Dhoni's endorsement career) observed in this context, "He is a World Cup – winning captain and has mass appeal. Being from Ranchi, he can connect with people from rural areas. Again, he is flamboyant guy and urban people can identify with him. We're now going ahead with only the top brands and have said no to at least 10 companies."

Celebrities are supposed to create a positive rub-off effect on products/services and thus help sponsors in selling their offerings. However, there is a certain time frame within which a celebrity's popularity and appeal needs to be leveraged by advertisers in order to reap the maximum benefit. Celebrities do have a control over their life span as brand endorsers. They need to be consistent performers in their professional domains and should be projecting a consistent image in the media. Celebrities need to be good media managers. Prathap Suthan, national creative director, Cheil, south-west Asia averred in this context, "Advertising is all about flamboyance, so the ambassador not just needs to be consistent in performance but should also portray himself or herself in a particular way in public." A very important ingredient that goes on to offer a prolonged endorsement career to a celebrity is his/her ability to reinvent. The reinvention could be in terms of one's personal grooming or it could be associating with some other domain of work apart from one's core profession. Sajid Shamim, director, marketing and product at Reebok India observed, "It's important for a brand ambassador to reinvent himself. David Beckham is a prime example. These days, though he does not play for the England team consistently, he is still a sought-after name." Reinvention has been in vogue among the Indian celebrities too. From Aamir Khan to Sachin Tendulkar, from Shah Rukh Khan to Hrithik Roshan, they all have made a conscious effort to reinvent themselves through personal grooming. Aamir Khan's long locks and big moustache at one point of time and then displaying cropped hair later or Sachin Tendulkar from being a clean shaven guy to the one sporting a French beard, these are all examples of how celebrities make a conscious effort to maintain the desirability quotient among the advertisers. There are also celebrities like Shah Rukh Khan who have in the last few years diversified from being just a leading actor in Bollywood to becoming a successful film producer with movies like Main Hoon Na and Om Shanti Om and an owner of an IPL (Indian Premier League) franchise named Kolkata Knight Riders. This diversification has been a way to reinvent him self as a celebrity as far as SRK is concerned. When Amitabh Bachchan appeared on Indian television as the anchor of the reality show, Kaun Banega Crorepati, it heralded good times for the mega star as a brand endorser. An iconic Bollywood actor of Bachchan's calibre turning into a television host was one of the most incredible and effective way to reinvent as a celebrity. Inability to reinvent one self often leads to loss of endorsement contracts for a celebrity. The replacement of movie star Fardeen Khan by Bollywood actors Saif Ali Khan, Esha Deol and Upen Patel by apparel brand, Provogue is an example to be cited in this context. Aarti Poddar, general manager- marketing, Provogue observed, "We opted for new ambassadors, as with Fardeen there wasn't anything new we could come up with. In five years, we had reached a point where all shoots looked the same."

There are few parameters that decide the market value of a celebrity viz. Celebrity mass appeal or popularity, celebrity image, celebrity's power to reinvent and of course the celebrity's performance in his professional domain. Apart from SRK and Big B who reportedly were the leading brand endorsers from the world of cinema and Sachin Tendulkar who was the star endorser from the cricketing fraternity in the year 2007, there have been number of other celebrities whose market worth have skyrocketed in recent times. Deepika Padukone, whose debut movie, Om Shanti Om has done wonders at the box-office is reportedly having a brand worth of INR 80 lakh which is five times the amount she was being offered prior to being introduced to the cine goers. M.S. Dhoni, who initially earned between INR 40 lakh to INR 60 lakh per endorsement (when he had long locks), is presently commanding six times that amount after going for a makeover and seeking incredible success as the Indian skipper. Saif Ali Khan's success with movies at the box-office coupled with his cool looks and his frequently changing style statement have been some of the factors behind his seeking INR 36 crore worth of endorsements a year. Anirban Blah, CEO Globosport revealed, "Saif's doing 12 endorsements and that roughly comes to about Rs 3 crore for each." Yuvraj Singh and Sourav Ganguly are some of the other cricketers who have earned significantly through brand endorsements. While Yuvraj made INR 2 crore per endorsement by endorsing brands like Reebok, Bentley, Westside, Pepsi etc., Sourav gained INR 1 crore to INR 1.5 crore per endorsement by endorsing Puma, Chirag Computers and TMT steel bars. Speaking about Sourav, Vinita Bangard, COO of Percept Talent Management observed, "Sourav's brand value may not be the same as it was when he was the captain of the Indian cricket team but people recognize that he was one of our most successful skippers. He is worth anywhere between Rs 8 and Rs 10 crore a year today, endorsing brands like Puma, Chirag Computers and TMT steel bars. We'll be seeing much more of him soon."

There are some definite reasons why only select few celebrities have been found to seek scores of endorsement contracts while many other celebrities have negligible number of brands to endorse. The lack of mass appeal for a celebrity, his/her inability to maintain a consistent image, his/her incapability to reinvent by way of grooming or diversifying into newer endeavours and last and most importantly a celebrity's inconsistent performance in his/her professional domain are some of the major factors that makes sponsors keep a safe distance from a majority of celebrities. It is only a select few celebrities who apart from being consistent doers in their profession make a conscious and effective effort to project themselves as 'hot' properties to the sponsors.

There are however certain risks involved with celebrity endorsements. The 'value mismatch' between a celebrity and the product/service to be endorsed can be one of them. The celebrity-target audience misfit can be another risk. One of the most important risks to be considered while going for celebrity endorsements is the celebrity controversy risk. Often, inconsistent performance of a celebrity in his/her professional domain or a scandal in the lives of celebrities impact endorsements negatively. The former instance happens more in case of sports personalities while the later is the part and parcel of most people from the world of entertainment. When a celebrity is extremely popular and endorses a number of brands, it becomes another major risk. In this context, Prathap Suthan opined, "At times the brand gets overshadowed by its endorser. So, it is good to have endorsers who are exclusive. Though they come with a high price tag, they bring exclusivity which is rare." Celebrities endorsing multiple brands often minimize the recall value for brands.

Many experts from the advertising fraternity believe that it is still the 'big idea' and not the celebrity charisma that does the trick for brands. The most outstanding example that can be cited in this context is the Vodafone ad featuring the pug. The ad is lovable and has very high recall value. In a survey conducted by IMRB, it was revealed that 78% of the Indians felt that the most important factor while buying a product is quality while only 3% attached greater importance to the celebrity endorsement factor. Further only 22% believed that the products endorsed by celebrities were actually used by them while 51% opined that celebrities endorsed brands just for the sake of big bucks. Another striking revelation was that 15% of the respondents had wrong brand recalls for Amitabh Bachchan and 9% had wrong brand recalls for Shah Rukh Khan.

Although, there are many who find little significance of celebrity endorsements and consider them as waste of big bucks, the trend seems to gather momentum with the passage of time. However, there is a strong debate that is emerging and that is between movie stars and cricketers, which is the most preferred category of celebrity for endorsements. Aarti Poddar of Provogue observed in this context, "As a creative person, I would say it depends on script and brand demands." Poddar was however found to be in favour of movie stars since in the case of cricketers, bouquets and brickbats are dependant on their present on-field performance. Sajid Shamim of Reebok India had a contrarian view as he averred, "Though film stars can be sued as models to showcase the products, it is sports stars who are part of the story."

References:
Kalla Avinash, "On the brandwagon!", The Times of India (Times Life!), March 2nd 2008
Basu Arpita, "What's The Big Deal?", The Times of India, March 5th 2008
Menon Sugatha, "Let's renounce star worship!", http://news.in.msn.com/columns/article.aspx?cp-documentid=1329990
"Celebrity endorsement ads on TV up 49% during 2007",
http://www.thehindubusinessline.com/2008/04/09/stories/2008040950750500.htm, April 9th 2008

Sourav Ganguly and the Interesting Case of Brand Endorsements

Over the years, Indian cricket has produced not just some outstanding cricketers but also some durable celebrity brands out of some of the players. With the meteoric rise of sports celebrity endorsement in India since the mid-1990s, there have been a number of cricketers who have neatly pocketed millions through brand endorsements. However, there have been cricketers like Sachin Tendulkar, Sourav Ganguly and Rahul Dravid who have not just represented India in international cricket for sufficiently long period of time but have also proved their efficiency as popular and credible brand endorsers. Among them, it has been Sourav Ganguly who has proved to be a 'fighter' brand both on and off the field. His cricketing career has seen many ups and downs, been subjected to many controversies but the brand has shown true resilience in guarding its equity and making a comeback of sorts whenever it seemed that the brand was down in the doldrums. Sourav Ganguly's passion, aggression and style as a player and his inspirational leadership skills have made him one of the most revered celebrity brands of Indian cricket.

Brand Ganguly: The Ups and Downs

Marketers felt that a lot of Sourav's brand value came from the fact that he was a successful and aggressive captain. Thus it was observed that brands which focused on the aggressive leadership aspect found Sourav Ganguly a perfect brand ambassador. Since 2000, Ganguly's image in the cricketing arena was reported to seek a major boost because of his fearless attitude and his almost immaculate leadership skills. More and more marketers thus tried to impart a fiery and stylish appeal to their brands by opting for Ganguly as their brand endorser.

In the context of endorsing beverages, Sourav was found to endorse Coca-Cola till 2002 before he switched to endorsing Pepsi. In 2003, after a three year contract with Percept D'Mark concluded, a tussle was reported between the said company and Nimbus, a sports production company to sign a deal with Sourav for managing his endorsement interests. There were reports that Nimbus had made an offer of Rs 60 crore for a period of five years. However, Harish Thawani, who was the cochairman of World Sports Nimbus said, "We have given no such proposal to Ganguly, nor are we contemplating to. There is no resolution even in the company board of taking cricketers on board for celebrity management." Sanjay Lal, the CEO and executive director at Percept D'Mark opined that the contract which his company signed with Ganguly in the year 2000 failed to ensure minimum guarantees for the cricket star. Further, there were reports that Ganguly was unhappy with the fact that Percept had generated about Rs 15 crore worth of contracts for him in a period of three years that was lower than what World Tel achieved for Sachin Tendulkar. Sachin could make Rs 20 crore per annum from brand endorsements. Lal said, "You must remember that we picked up Sourav Ganguly when cricket was going through a bad phase – the game as well as cricket stars were scam tainted and people were losing faith in the game." But then, Percept did the needful to ensure the continuity of their business relationship with Sourav. Sanjay Lal said, "We have matched our rival's offer and the paperwork with Sourav Ganguly should be completed by the end of the week." He added, "The basic reason for Sourav Ganguly to consider a fresh offer was money and we have been able to match that." As per the new contract, Percept ensured Sourav a basic minimum guarantee of Rs 48 crore over a five-year period. It was essential for Percept to fetch an additional Rs 5 crore worth of business per year which was not perceived to be a challenge by Lal as he said, "Hypothetically speaking, we will need to get him six contracts worth Rs 1.5 crore per annum, which is not such a great challenge." Lal added, "We will do some innovative promotions for him to meet the minimum guarantee terms." Sourav's endorsement contracts for several brands like Hero Honda, Pepsi, ESPN, Sahara and LG were up for renewal and it was believed an amount of Rs 1.2 crore that Sourav was making per annum per brand might be hiked to Rs 2 crore per contract. Apart from the above mentioned brands, Sourav was also found to endorse brands like Britannia Tiger biscuits, Tata Indicom and Himani Sona Chandi Chyawanprash .

After the 2003 World Cup and India's subsequent tour of Australia, Sourav's performance as a batsman was found to reach its nadir which continued for quite some time. His consistent poor form both in tests as well as in ODIs raised doubts about Ganguly's future tenure as a captain and it was further felt that his place in the Indian squad was insecure. Sourav Ganguly's poor performance seemed to affect his saleability as a brand. The future of 'Brand Ganguly' seemed to be in jeopardy. Reacting to the poor performance of Ganguly on field and its probable impact on Sourav as a brand endorser, Sanjay Lal said, "We are waiting for his good form to return before we sign any fresh deals. He is going through a bad patch, so obviously we are not doing any active marketing for him." Lal was found to be quite optimistic about Sourav as a cricketer when he said, "A player like Ganguly will not be shaken by one bad patch." He further observed, "The cricketer is already packed and we can add just one or two more endorsements." In early 2005, when the Pakistan cricket team toured India and Ganguly was banned for six matches, it was reported that LG's Rs 60 crore commercial series titled 'khelega kya' went off air. The ads featured Ganguly and his Pakistani counterpart Inzamam-ul-Haq taking on each other as medieval warlords.

However, Salil Kapoor, former marketing head at LG said, "The 'khelega kya' contest is on only till April 20. So we are not pulling out because Ganguly has been banned for the next six matches." Girish V Rao, vice- president (Sales) at LG had similar opinions when he said, "The contracts of all our cricketing brand ambassadors ended in November. This includes Sourav Ganguly and we are not planning to renew these contracts for now. We will take a call on signing on sporting brand ambassadors after our financial year ends in December." Reacting to Ganguly's termination of endorsement contract with LG, Shailendra Singh, managing director at Percept D'Mark said, "The company has not replaced him with anybody else. At present LG is not taking on any new endorsement contracts, so it would be unfair to say that this is a setback for Ganguly." Abdul Khan, vice-president (Marketing), Tata Indicom opined on an optimistic note, "This is just a phase. There are ups and downs in everyone's lives. Two-match ban, six-match ban...these are just technicalities. He has been our brand ambassador for one-and-a-half years now. What he brings to the brand is his iconic status, his aggressiveness, his attitude of encouraging young talent and of knitting the team together. We don't see any negative impact on the brand."

Sourav's consistent poor performance not only triggered his loss of captaincy but also his removal from 'Team India'. In the ten months that he was out of the Indian team, Ganguly's brand endorsement contracts were reported to dry up. For a brief period he was seen to endorse Pogo chips26. Ganguly, who endorsed nine brands at one point of time, was left with just four in his kitty, which were Hero Honda, Reid & Taylor, Sahara and Pepsi. However, Vineeta Bangar, vicepresident of Percept's strategic business arm Celebrity Management Services said, "none of them pulled out but the companies just decided to change focus." Bangar's opinion seemed to have substance going by what Aditya Agarwal, Director, Emami said, "We are sure that Ganguly would make a comeback in the test series and subsequently find place in the one day squad as well. We have not stopped featuring him in the ads for Sona Chandi. In fact, during the India- South Africa match in Kolkata, we came out with ads stating Dada, we are with you." However, Agrawal also said, "We will take a call on extending his contract after his tenure is over." In 2006, Pepsi came up with 'The Blue Billion' campaign that was built around the former skipper's fallen status. The ad featured a forlorn Ganguly who said that he hoped that people had not forgotten him. The former skipper was found to express his resolve to comeback into the Indian squad. He also said that if however he could not make it, like the billion cricket lovers in India, he too will be cheering 'Team India' with the slogan 'Ooh aah India, Aaya India'. Sourav's cricket academy at Salt Lake City in Kolkata witnessed a cash crunch in 2006 as its sponsor; Videocon seemed like giving out discordant signals about their extent of financial commitment towards the training centre.

In November 2006, after Dilip Vengsarkar replaced Kiran More as the chairman of the National Selection Committee, Sourav Ganguly was recalled into the national squad for the three-test series against South Africa in South Africa. The decision was based on Ganguly's good performance in domestic cricket and also after India could not make it into the semis of the Champions Trophy that was held in India. The team also failed to win the three opening games of the ODI series in South Africa. The selectors backed Ganguly's experience as they felt that he would be instrumental in bringing about a turnaround in 'Team India's' performance.

Brand Sourav: The Revival

With Sourav's successful comeback in international cricket, companies were found to make a beeline for him to endorse their brands. Expressing her opinion regarding the comeback of 'Brand Ganguly' Vinita Bangar, vice-president at Percept D'Mark opined that none of the corporate deserted Ganguly for his poor performance and his subsequent omission for the Indian squad but they had actually acted as per their business priorities. Citing the examples of LG and Emami, she said, "LG and Emami did move away, but that was more to do with their business decision to look away from cricketers." In the context of Ganguly's brand endorsement prospects since his comeback she observed, "However, following his comeback, things have changed and we have received enquiries from various corporate and are in talks with 4-5 big companies who want to sign up Ganguly." She further said, "He has come back with a bang and he is the only player, we feel, who identifies with young India." One major development that was reported since Ganguly's comeback was that Videocon had no further hesitation in continuing with their financial commitment towards Sourav's cricket academy in Kolkata. "All the misunderstandings were sorted out as soon as Sourav was recalled into the Indian squad in South Africa. After that, everything has been uphill for Dada", opined an official of the academy.

Soon after his international comeback, the global electronics brand, TCL was one of the first to sign an endorsement deal with Sourav along with S. Sreesanth, the Indian fast bowler who seemed quite promising on India's tour to South Africa. It was reported that the amount involved in the TCL deal was in the Rs 1-2 crore range with Ganguly accounting for a major chunk. The two cricketers were signed for a period of 1 year with the option for an extension. It was further learnt that Coca Cola was in the process of wooing Sourav back for endorsements. There were speculations of a successful outcome in that context since Ganguly was unhappy with the short-term contact that Pepsi was offering him at that juncture. Ganguly's brand value was estimated to be between Rs 1- 1.25 crore with brand endorsements for Pepsi, Hero Honda, Reid & Taylor and Tata Indicom in his kitty. Another important endorsement deal with Sourav was signed by Puma Sports India Limited, the Indian subsidiary of the Germany-based sports lifestyle brand Puma. Speaking on the occasion, Rajiv Mehta, MD, Puma Sports India Limited opined, "Genius has no youth, but all starts with the ripeness of age and experience. Ganguly is a perfect prototype of this." The contract was for a period of one year and as per the deal, Ganguly was supposed to don the company's footwear and apparel during all his on-field appearances within the contract period. When Ganguly was asked regarding his future endorsement prospects, he said, "I am being approached by many other companies to be their model, but, I think this is the time to concentrate on cricket." He added, "Frankly speaking, if runs keep coming, the rest will follow.

Commenting on 'Brand Ganguly's' resurgence, a Percept spokesperson said, "After sealing the deals with Puma and TCL, we are on the verge of signing up Sourav with a bank and an IT hardware company. With his current form and the expectations lying on him, the companies will not think twice." In the context of 'Brand Ganguly's' comeback, a Sahara official observed, "His resurgence in light of some key batsmen failing assumes more significance and if current comparative forms can be considered as an indicator, then Brand Sourav is definitely back and that too with a vengeance. He has actually risen like a phoenix." Soon after Ganguly's praiseworthy performance in South Africa Shailendra Singh, MD, Percept D'Mark observed, "After being down and out Brand Sourav, therefore, is back in business. Beverage companies are back in conversation and two fresh deals involving a consumer electronics and a real estate company could be signed immediately on his return." He further opined, "The Sourav story – leader to underdog to performer – is all about drama and companies just love that kind of a combination." Singh felt that Sourav's rate per endorsement was most likely to increase in the immediate future. On an optimistic note, brand consultant, Jagdeep Kapoor said, "He may have been going through a difficult patch but his brand value was never down. His performance in the current series has only toughened the brand and its value can therefore only go up." Ad man, Piyush Pandey, while commenting on the comeback of 'Brand Ganguly' observed, "There are good days ahead of him. As human beings we always appreciate the underdog in some way. He exemplifies the spirit of not being bogged down in any situation."[42] For ad man, Prahlad Kakkar, the comeback of Sourav as a cricketer as well as a brand ambassador was quite natural. Expressing his opinion, Kakkar said, "Everybody salutes the rising sun and the same thing has happened with Sourav. It is not at all surprising." Harish Bijoor, CEO, Harish Bijoor Consultants however had a different take so far as the resurgence of 'Brand Ganguly' was concerned. Bijoor opined, "To me Sourav reached his peak when he took off his shirt at Lord's after India thrashed England in 2002. His peak is over. Ditto for his advertising revenues. It's going to be difficult for him to regain that image. He stands for what he has been. Regional brands like Boroline and Deys Medical might suit him now, not a Reebok or a Nike."

References:
Sarkar John & Mukherjee Shubham, "Brand Ganguly back in business",
http://economictimes.indiatimes.com/articleshow/1077600.cms
http://cricket.indiatimes.com/Sections/News/Sourav_the_darling_of_corporate_world/articleshow/1695100.cms
http://en.wikipedia.org/wiki/Sourav_Ganguly
http://content-www.cricinfo.com/wc2007/content/story/133735.html
Bansal Shuchi, "Ganguly, Percept set to resume innings",
http://inhome.rediff.com/money/2003/oct/01spec.htm, October 1st 2003
Bhushan Ratna, "Brand Sourav's selling power dips",
http://timesofindia.indiatimes.com/articleshow/1077082.cms, April 14th 2005
Subramanian Nithya & Kaushik Neha, "Sourav remains brand endorser, but new offers have to wait",http://www.thehindubusinessline.com/2005/04/14/stories/2005041401520400.htm, April 14th 2005
Brand Ganguly caught in the gully!",
http://www.thehindubusinessline.com/2005/12/02/stories/2005120204030800.htm, December 2nd

2005

"Advertisers make beeline for Ganguly",
http://timesofindia.inidiatimes.com/articleshow/1084174.cms
http://cricket.indiatimes.com/Sections/News/Sourav_the_darling_of_corporate_world/articleshow/1695100.cms
Jawed Zeeshan, "Sourav's back, so is sponsor",
http://www.telegraphindia.com/1070224/asp/nation/story_7434714.asp, February 24th 2007
"Puma signs up Sourav", http://www.financialexpress.com/fe_full_story.php?content_id=155959
http://cricket.indiatimes.com/Sections/News/Sourav_the_darling_of_corporate_world/articleshow/1695100.cms
http://souravganguly.net/endorsements.htm
http://welovesourav.com

Fragrances and Celebrities: Understanding the Correlation

For quite sometime, fragrance makers across the globe have been found to leverage on the popularity of celebrity brands to capture market share for their brands. However, it will be wrong to state over here that it has been fragrance makers who have only gained from this exercise. The stars who have either lent their names to brands or who have endorsed a particular fragrance brand have equally been benefited. Its because of this symbiotic business relationship that the global celebrity fragrance industry is worth $1 billion. Some of the most recognized international brands being Instinct, Darling, Curious, Glow by Jlo, White Diamonds, etc.

While Instinct as a perfume brand is associated with the internationally acclaimed footballer, David Beckham; Darling has been endorsed by the international pop diva, Kylie Minogue. Glow and Still by Jlo are another two celebrity fragrance brands that have been associated with international pop sensations. Curious is a brand endorsed by Britney Spears while Glow by JLo is a brand associated with Jennifer Lopez. White Diamonds is a brand that was introduced by the veteran Hollywood actress, Elizabeth Taylor in 1991.

It has been observed that over the years, fragrances as a product category have evolved from having just a functional appeal to one having tremendous aspirational value. The fragrance brands have by and large appealed to the teenagers and the youth among whom big aspirations are almost habitual. Although there have been some who have dismissed the significance of celebrities as far as the success of fragrance brands are concerned and have further highlighted the imminent risks involved in celebrity endorsements, the positive impact of celebrities on fragrance brands have been widely accepted.

Fragrances: Changing Consumer Perceptions

It has been observed that the association of celebrities with fragrance brands has been primarily due to changing consumer behavior over the years. From being considered as products that make one smell good, fragrances have been recognized by consumers globally as an expression of an entire personality, a way to feel different. Fragrances have been considered by many as a means to merge fantasy with reality. Lippi Lal (Lal), a Mumbai-based fragrance consultant opined, "There is a sub-conscious reason why we wear a perfume – it is to express ourselves; either to enhance who we are or to portray who we want to be. As for celebrities, they embody the perfection we want to achieve in our own lives. When you buy a celebrity scent and wear it, for a while, you are a part of the world of that celebrity and it becomes an aspirational moment." Mumbai-based Rohit Gothi of Lornamead Personal Care, while substantiating what Lal stated observed, "Earlier, fragrances were meant to be so overpowering that others would recognize them. But as tastes and the consumer choices evolved, today, they are much more personal. Each brand tries to give a character and soul to a fragrance. For instance, you might have a role model like Shah Rukh Khan and buy a fragrance named after him, or buy a perfume called Jaipur that captures the soul of a city for you."

It has been reported that celebrity endorsed fragrances have attracted the 16-24 years old consumer segment the most. Almost one in five in this segment owns a celebrity fragrance as per TGI. Commenting on the said consumer segment, Wendy Liebmann (Liebmann), president of WSL Strategic Retail observed, "Just like younger people like to experiment in their personal lives with dating different people, it is the same thing with fashion, music, even perfumes. They want what is hot right now." Fragrances as a product category have witnessed a major shift in buying and consuming trends since the 1990s because of which it was reported that there was a major dip in the sale of fragrances in the early 2000s. It was reported by the market research firm NPD Group that in 2003, global sales of fragrances was \$2.8 billion which was 2% less than the total global sales in 2002. Commenting on the declining sales trend, Liebmann observed, "The business has been very difficult for the last five to six years. A change in consumer trends is partly to blame." He further observed, "In the past, a single fragrance had a life cycle of may be six to seven years, because people would stay loyal to a scent for a longer period of time. The life cycle is much shorter now, especially with the younger consumers, who always want the latest product."

However it was the world's largest fragrance maker, Coty which heralded the silver lining for the global fragrance business in 2002 when it introduced the perfume – Glow by JLo. Jennifer Lopez also known as JLo was the celebrity behind the fragrance.

Celebrity Fragrances: A Lucrative Marketing Proposition

Glow by JLo was not the first major instance of a celebrity endorsing a perfume brand. In the early 1990s, it was the veteran Hollywood actress Elizabeth Taylor who was the face of the White Diamonds perfume. Although Taylor's movie career had faded significantly at that point of time, she was still a popular personality in the Hollywood fraternity. She commanded a loyal fan base which was proved later as the White Diamonds perfume went on to become one of the most successful celebrity fragrances with more than \$1 billion in sales.

The celebrity fragrance business has been observed to be a win-win proposition for both celebrities as well as the companies . The multi-billion dollar business has reportedly been a lucrative opportunity for the celebrities to mint money. The initiative has also been found to be a profitable proposition for the fragrance makers across the globe. The concept has attracted celebrities from various professional domains to endorse the fragrance brands. From recording artists to best-selling authors; from sportspersons to designers, all have been a part of this 'scent-sational' revolution. Since the successful launch of Glow by JLo in 2002, there has been a spurt in the number of celebrity fragrances that have been launched. Coty has gone on to unveil several other perfumes related to Jennifer Lopez like Miami Glow, Still and Live. Another international pop diva who has lent her name and endorsed a brand named Darling is Kylie Minogue (**Exhibit-I**). It has been reported that the Lopez family of perfumes earns more than \$100 million yearly for Coty. Coty has signed several other internationally renowned celebrities like Sarah Jessica Parker, Shania Twain and David Beckham. Besides Coty, there have been other companies like Elizabeth Arden, which hired Hollywood actresses like Elizabeth Taylor and Catherine Zeta Jones; Chanel that signed Hollywood actress Nicole Kidman and Estee Lauder who have successfully joined the bandwagon of celebrity fragrance makers.

Exhibit-I

An Advertisement of Minogue's Darling

It is not that only Hollywood actresses and international pop divas have created waves across the globe by endorsing fragrance brands and lending their names to perfumes. Similar trends have been observed among the Indian celebrities too. Lata eau de parfum has been endorsed by Bharat Ratna Lata Mangeshkar. Zeenat is a perfume promoted by yesteryear actress of Bollywood, Zeenat Aman. Shah Rukh Khan has also got a perfume in his name called SK and so does Shilpa Shetty (S2) (**Exhibit-II**)

Exhibit-II
Indian Celebrities Endorsing Fragrances

One aspect that decides the viability of a celebrity to endorse a perfume or to lend his or her name to it is the popularity of the celebrity. He or she should have huge appeal among his audiences. The celebrity needs to be an inspiration to many and there should be many who aspire to be like the celebrity. The above has been found to be true for almost all celebrities till date who have endorsed fragrance brands. From Elizabeth Taylor to Jennifer Lopez, from Celine Dion to Mariah Carey, from Lata Mangeshkar to Shah Rukh Khan, they all have a huge fan following and have been a source of inspiration to millions. Fragrance makers have even been found to sign endorsement contracts with rising stars. Such strategy have many times worked in their favor where the companies are able to make the most out of a brand with a relatively short period of time by cashing in one the hysteria surrounding an upcoming celebrity. After winning her maiden Wimbledon title, Maria Sharapova was reportedly signed in to endorse certain perfume brands. Similar was the case with Shilpa Shetty after her incredible win in the internationally acclaimed reality show Celebrity Big Brother. She went on to promote a brand of perfume named after her, S2. Another global phenomenon that has often been observed is that the perfume makers sign celebrities for brand endorsements with the objective of emphasizing the target market for the brand. Thus Coty signed Celine Dion to target the women in their mid-30s; Mary Kate and Ashley Olsen were signed to attract the tween segment while Shania Twain was signed to appeal to the country-music lovers.

The fragrance marketers have found the alliance quite lucrative over the years. Huge costs are involved in building a perfume brand tight from the scratch which is taken care of when a popular celebrity gets associated with it. Candace Corlett of WSL Strategic Retail opines in this context, "Building a fragrance brand name from start, without any affiliation, is a very expensive proposition. A much quicker route to sales is to borrow a star's identity." Celebrity endorsed fragrances have often been found to rake in the moolah for the marketers at much quicker pace. Britney Spear's Curious as a brand was reported to earn $100 million in the very first year of its launch. It was reported that in the UK, sales of celebrity fragrances increased by 2000% since 2004. The global market for premium fragrances generates $18.7 billion in sales which includes a significant chunk of celebrity fragrances.

17

Looking from a Different Perspective

One of the major limitations associated with the business of celebrity fragrances is that brands are largely dependant on the popularity of the celebrity as far as their shelf lives are concerned. Till the time, the celebrity has a huge fan following and enjoys popularity amongst his aficionados, the perfume brand sells like hot cakes and consumers are willing to pay the premium for acquiring the brand but the moment, the celebrity gains negative publicity concerning his or her personal or professional life, it spells doom for the brand he or she is associated with. Commenting on the helplessness of companies as far as controlling the negative ripple effect on brands is concerned, Elizabeth Montgomery of equity research firm SG Cowen observed, "If you're selling a personality, you can't control whether an actress gets a front-page divorce." Recovery of costs becomes a paramount problem due to the forced shorter life cycle of the brand. Brands need to have a minimum shelf life of more than year to justify the astronomical costs involved while launching them. Marketers often foresee that a perfume brand will rake in the profits before a celebrity ceases to be successful and popular and will also establish itself in the minds of buyers but that does not happen all the time and a costly launch often has been found to get lost in the brand clutter.

It has been further observed that the 'celebrity halo effect' often fails to capture the imagination of a majority of consumers and also certain segments of perfume makers. Neerja Marwaha, a Mumbai-based blender of exotic signature perfumes opines, "I believe that perfume can attract money, love or power. But I'm totally put off by celebrities lending their names to a perfume. I want a perfume that goes with my unique body chemistry. A fragrance should transport you to another world, so that you can express who you are and what you want to be." Like Marwaha, there are many who believe in the quality of a perfume and are least willing to submit themselves to the marketing gimmicks associated with celebrity fragrances. Delhi-based Tikka Shatrujit Singh, who works closely with premium brands like Louis Vuitton observes, "Many of the old and classic fragrances did not have any celebs endorsing them. Like Shalimar in India or Joy by Jean Patou, but they were classics and still are. Today, we live in an era of celebrities and we imagine that if a big name is attached to a perfume, it must be good. But I personally feel that many of the new perfumes cannot be compared to those of the past."

In a 2007 Euromonitor International report titled "The World Market for Cosmetics and Toileteries", it has been predicted that the global sales of celebrity endorsed perfumes is set to decline significantly by the year 2010. In the US, where celebrity endorsed fragrances had witnessed significant sales since 2002, it has been forecasted that the sales of fragrances will decline by 25% by the year 2010 and the celebrities will loose their impact as far as promoting fragrance brands are concerned. The report mentions several other problem areas like the over saturation of the celebrity fragrances in the global market. Since the success of Glow by JLo in 2002, various global perfume makers have launched a plethora of celebrity fragrances that have caused severe brand clutter. Moreover, in order to keep up with the image of the celebrity, perfume ranges are being consistently revamped which is further adding to the clutter. For example, if Coty's JLo collection is taken into account, one finds that the company has launched several new fragrances from time to time like Miami Glow, Still and Live. Diana Dodson (Dodson), senior industry analyst at Euromonitor International observes, "With so many new releases, manufacturers are running the risk that consumers will become increasingly confused and frustrated by the never-ending choice."

Celebrity Fragrances: What Lies Ahead?

The 2007 Euromonitor International report suggests that the global fragrance manufacturers should concentrate on the quality of the products as that will soon be the driving force in future. In this context, Dodson opines, "The fragrances market has strong potential for growth if manufacturers can find ways to pull customers towards 'quality', rather than selling on image alone. As part of this move towards premium products, ingredients will play a more central role." The report also suggests marketers to develop such business strategies which will make customers use fragrances more frequently during a day. The fragrance makers need to come up with new and more portable fragrance formats like roller-balls. Strong and relevant differentiation needs to be established among the brands. Experts opine that fragrance makers should position their brands such that they occupy a distinct space in the consumer's perceptual territory. However, there are some brand experts like Harish Bijoor (Bijoor), CEO of Harish Bijoor Consultants who opine that the multi-billion dollar fragrance market needs celebrities to 'create a retail heaven'. Bijoor observes, "Any thought is a brand and it can be physical or emotional. A fragrance is a sensory thought and when you use big stars for a brand, they bring their own string of associations. This is called 'emotive appeal branding'. It is a clever marketing strategy to the extent that most people emote positively to a star and there is a positive emotional connect instantly."

References:

Boorstin Julia, "The Scent of Celebrity",
http://money.cnn.com/magazines/fortune/fortune_archive/2005/11/14/8360679/index.htm, November 14th
2005
Chowdary Asha, "More than just a nose job!",
http://www.ajitweekly.com/ajitweekly2/PDF_NEW/THE_CON/26_Oct_2007/12.pdf, October 2007
"Celebrity-endorsed perfumes on the rise",
http://economictimes.indiatimes.com/articleshow/2484543.cms, October 24th 2007
Bhatnagar Pariia, "Celebrities take scent-er stage",
http://money.cnn.com/2004/11/18/news/newsmakers/celebrity_perfume/index.htm, November 19th
2004
"Celebrity fragrances have limited shelf life",
http://www.marketresearchworld.net/index.php?option=com_content&task=view&id=1182&Itemid=48

The Making of 'Youth' Brands

"What makes India's youth worth studying is evident; one of the world's hottest economies, a billion people, roughly half of them between the ages of 15 and 29 years, and rising purchasing power. It is a demographic gold mine for marketers and a case-study-in- progress of democratic capitalism."

Source: Businessworld, November 6th 2006

India is a predominantly young nation when compared to countries like the USA and the UK with 55% of its population falling in the youth bracket. About 450 million individuals in India are estimated to be below 20 years of age. 105 million in the age group of 15-19 are already in their early years of discretionary consumption. It is these Generation Xers who are contributing heavily to the rapid change in the Indian economy and are fast becoming the darling of India Inc. The proliferation of the foreign television channels like MTV and other movie channels have exposed the Indian youth to the western style of living and thought in a big way. The emergence of English as a common language and the importance attached to it in the Indian society have also been found to yield rich dividends not only in the context of the careers of the Indian youth but also it has indirectly made a marketer's task of successfully targeting this segment a lot easier. The mushrooming of BPOs in India and the fat pay packets offered by them to a large chunk of the Indian youth populace has been another reason why the marketers have found this segment to be an increasingly lucrative proposition.

"The underlying factor making Generation Y an ever attractive demographic is its growing purchasing power. The trend is being fuelled by higher disposable incomes resulting from more generous allowances and teens opting to work part-time during schooling, less reliance on parents to make purchases, and heightened media awareness", observes Anil Jain, General Manager(BD&NC), BSNL. Across various industries, it has been found that successful marketers do not predict any fashion or trend while targeting the youth; rather they follow the segment diligently. They identify the opinion leaders, identify with them and make an effective attempt to understand what excites them. Accordingly, they position their products or services. Successful marketers incorporate specific elements in their product mix, communication and branding strategies such that they effectively target both the 'Coconuts' and the 'Cappuccinos' sub- segments of the Indian youth [**Exhibit I**] or else relevantly appeal to either one of them.

Exhibit- I

Conflicting Behavioral Patterns of the Indian Youth

Confused Generation?

COCONUTS: 'Brown on the outside, white on the inside'. Indians who adopt western mannerisms and ways of living. While remaining proud of their 'brown' exterior and the country of their birth, they hold an open-minded attitude, not held back by the rigidity of tradition.

CAPPUCCINOS: 'White on the surface but brown below'. Indians who seem to have adopted a western way of life but deep down are fundamentally Indian, believing strongly in Indian traditions without considering changing or modernising them.

A post-mortem analysis of five of India's leading brands who have strongly identified themselves with the Indian youth either since their inception or during subsequent stages of their life-cycle through innovative, relevant product offerings and branding strategies will substantiate the fact.

Close up:
Close up, a brand from the HLL stable, was the first brand in India targeting the youth in the oral care market. It was the first gel toothpaste in India and also the first toothpaste with mouthwash. It was observed to be a truly challenger brand in the context of toothpastes as it carved a distinct identity for itself right at the outset based on its physical attributes and packaging. For the first time, people had the option to brush with transparent, shiny and bright red toothpaste. The paste further tasted good due to the presence of the spicy and icy mouthwash in it. For the youth, who were the prime focus of the brand, brushing in mornings was no longer a mundane affair after they used Close up. In a world of white pastes, Close up captured the consumers' perceptual territory as a bright red toothpaste. While the white pastes have calcium carbonate as a principal ingredient, Close up has silica, which is considered a more efficient abrasive that offers better cleaning of teeth. Unlike other toothpastes in the market that offered cavity control and strong teeth, Close up offered the cosmetic benefits of fresh breath and shiny white teeth. It was based on the consumer insight that people are conscious of how their breath smells only when they are quite close with people especially people from the opposite sex. The dual benefits of fresh breath and white teeth allowed people to get rid of their insecurity regarding bad breath and get close to each other. Close up's packaging was also found to be quite vibrant, energized and innovative since its launch in India. It has been the only toothpaste pack that features a warm Close up couple that imparts a distinct identity to any Close up pack in the cluttered Indian retail milieu .

Disruptive, differentiated, emotional, energetic and focused were found to be some of the prominent qualities of the Close up brand. While the brand stayed loyal to the core brand values of fun and romance, it constantly reinvented the way Close up couples were projected from time to time. Many feel that Close up was the first brand that showed smart modern girls who stood up for themselves and seemed smarter than their male counterparts on many occasions. The forward looking approach adopted by the brand mirrored the revolution in terms of women's liberation in mass media that took place in due course of time.

Over the years, it has been observed that while Close up has upheld the value of balancing pleasure and performance, the brand has operated on the values of innovation of authenticity. The brand has also been found to reposition itself with the changing times and social values. In the late 1980s, when Close up found that its upmarket imagery of boy-girl intimacy was clashing with the conservative Indian values, it retained the functional and emotional promise while the romance was given a more regional and traditional touch. A user/non-user format was used in the television commercials in the said period to reinforce the credentials of the brand. The period saw the creation of one of the most memorable commercials where the protagonists self-checked for fresh breath by blowing out 'ha-ha'. Moreover, when he smiled, a sparkle would appear on his teeth along with a distinct 'ting' sound. The brand was also found to feature cricket stars as brand endorsers to keep alive the youthful imagery associated with the brand. Thus Ajay Jadeja and Sourav Ganguly were found to endorse the brand that not only boosted the youth appeal and relevance but also ensured that the market share for the brand soared.

In the context of brand association strategies adopted by Close up, it was observed that though the brand retained its youthful persona, it made a successful attempt to cut across all demographics and in the process appeal to a wider cross-section of Indian demography. Thus the brand associated with Zee TV's Antakshari, a television program where teams competed with each other singing clips of Hindi film songs. Though it were the youth in colleges who participated in a major way in the program, people of other age groups and profession were also seen to take an active interest in the program and participate in it. Over the years, Close up has very creatively established itself in key places where consumers need fresh breath the most to aid really close interactions. All corner seats in various cinema halls, for instance, are branded 'Closeup Corners'. As per the market research agency ORG, the 1990s witnessed a substantial increment in Close up's value share from 15% at the beginning of the decade to 21% by the year 1999. Despite being a gel toothpaste with predominantly cosmetic benefits to talk about, Close up has been the toothpaste that has been ranked the 10th most trusted brand in India and also has been the leader in the gel segment for over 25 years as per an ORG survey. It has been widely felt that Close up has weaved its success story around the Indian youth by diligently customizing its product attributes and branding strategies to suit the temperaments of the said segment.

Hero Honda:

Hero Honda has been another brand in the Indian context that has continuously adopted product and branding strategies specifically targeted at the youth. It started as a joint venture in 1984 between the Hero Group of India and the Honda Group of Japan. Over the years, the Hero Honda bikes have proved to be the cynosure of the youth especially because of their style and fuel efficiency. The extensive range of bikes at the Hero Honda stable reveal that there has been a continuous, in-depth and relevant segmentation of India's youth population. There is a model for every possible and relevant customer segment. Based on the purchase criteria, there are three broad segments. In the 'Price' segment, where customers prioritize price over fuel efficiency, there are two sub-brands viz. CD Dawn and CD 100. In the 'Deluxe' segment, where customers seek product styling and fuel efficiency, Hero Honda has two subbrands, Splendor Plus and Passion Plus. The segment comprises 55% of the total motorcycle market. In the 'Premium' segment, where power and product styling are the deciding criteria, Ambition, CBZ and Karizma are the various models at the Hero Honda stable. Primarily, though any brand of bike targets the youth segment in a major way, Hero Honda has been a brand that has differentiated itself in the market by offering the youth meaningful value additions in terms of products and after-sales services. After emphasizing on the 3S factors (Sales, Service and Spares), Hero Honda included a fourth 'S' in the form of Safety. At select dealerships, Hero Honda created safety corners where customers who came to take delivery of their bikes, were explained the nuances of safe driving. The move was adopted by the brand since it was felt that in an ambience of increasing product parity, it were the 'soft services' that would differentiate a brand from its competitors. In order to appeal to a wider cross-section of the Indian youth, Hero Honda has in recent years adopted the brand gendering strategy. One such model that has been launched based on this strategy is Pleasure that has features and styling keeping the modern and up-market Indian female population in mind. Pleasure is a type of scooter from Hero Honda aimed mainly at the young working women of today and has the tagline- 'Why should boys have all the fun'. Lately, Hero Honda has launched some specialized retail outlets exclusively for women which have been named 'Just 4 Her'. The outlets have all female staff catering to the needs and requirements of the female customers. Hero Honda was one of the first motorcycle brands in India that strongly advocated for environment-friendly automobiles on the Indian roads through its 'We Care' campaign. In the process, it supported and acted positively in the context of one of the major issues of concern to the Indian youth and that is environment pollution. The 'Hero Honda Passport Program' has been another strategy adopted by Hero Honda to establish a more durable brand image in the minds of the Indian youth. The program has the tagline- 'Rishta Dil Ka', a slogan with a distinct youth appeal. The subsequent success of the program has confirmed the emotional association between Hero Honda and its customers.

In the context of communication strategies, Hero Honda has over the years produced various memorable youth-centric commercials. The very first such commercial was launched in 1984 that had the tagline, 'Fill it. Shut it. Forget it.' The tagline had an essentially youthful attitude associated with it. The commercial featured a young couple enjoying a ride on a CD 100. In 2001, when Passion was launched by Hero Honda, the ads had the headline- 'Born in a Studio. Not in a Factory', which again emphasized on the styling aspect associated with Hero Honda bikes that was a major differentiator when it came to youth appeal. Another tagline adopted by Hero Honda for its CD Dawn bikes that had that predominantly youthful flavor was 'Public Ka Naya Transport'. One tagline that has been quite successful in appealing to a wider cross-section of the Indian populace apart from the youth has been 'Andaz Nayi. Bharosa Wohi' adopted for the Splendor Plus bikes from Hero Honda which projects both the father and son relying heavily on the Splendor brand of bikes. In recent times, Hero Honda has associated with various activities and events that have been targeted at the youth. The brand has been sponsoring cricket tournaments and also cricket gears of the Indian cricketers. It was the one of the sponsors of the 2003 ICC cricket World Cup. It also sponsored the Sa Re Ga Ma Pa Show on Zee TV that had young talented singers from across the country competing to get the 'India Ki Voice' title. Hero Honda has associated with MTV for its Roadies Show, a reality show on MTV specifically for the adventurous youth. In the context of celebrity endorsements, Hero Honda has signed various youth icons of the nation from time to time like film star Hrithik Roshan and cricketer Sourav Ganguly .

'Desh Ki Dhadkan' has been the most significant and continuously used tagline of Hero Honda that very strongly appeals to the youth. Any nation thrives on the strength of its youth and by projecting its brand as a 'youth' brand, an immediate and long-lasting bond with the country's youth gets established. Hero Honda has established itself as one of the world's largest selling motorcycles. Three million bikes were sold in the year 2005-2006.

Titan FasTrack:
FasTrack, as a watch brand was launched by Titan Industries in 1998 and was positioned as 'Cool watches from Titan'. It came with a heavy fashion quotient and had that undeniable youth appeal. It became a Rs 25 crore brand by 2001-2002. But then sales were found to stagnate. Despite constantly refreshing the designs, sales for the brand did not improve when it was discovered that the problem lay with pricing. The college going youth that was the prime target of the brand could not afford the watches that were priced higher than Rs 1000. The FasTrack watches were priced between Rs 1200 and Rs 2700 that did not encourage too many repeat purchases. In 2004, the FasTrack brand of watches was relaunched as India's first youth-oriented watch brand. Speaking on the occasion, Mr. Bijou Kurien, former COO – Watches, at Titan said, "Today's youth lives in an instant gratification era. They are ambitious, demanding more out of life – constantly seeking excitement in everything. This generation refuses to be bogged down by one thing for too long. FasTrack, lends itself to this variety seeking attitude of today's youth through a new product range that is innovatively styled, boldly designed and distinctly provocative." The FasTrack range of watches was unveiled based on extensive research concerning the products, lifestyles and attitudes of the 15-25 year olds. Major reworking was done on the price front.FasTrack, in its earlier avatar were watches that had a steely look and were sturdy and long-lasting. But then based on consumer research, the company found that watches made of plastic and bright colors were the ones that were most preferable to the college goers. In short, it was found

that the target segment was more concerned about the look and styling of watches rather than the material .

In 2004, Titan went for brand extension in the context of its FasTrack range. With the launch of FasTrack Eye Gear in 2004, the brand extended to sunglasses. Eyewear was a logical extension for the brand as was put forth by Harminder P Sahni, the COO at KSA Technopak, "FasTrack is addressing the same consumer for both watches and sunglasses because both products are about style and not function, whereas something like a handbag is both functional and stylish." "We want to give young people a fashionable product of good quality that is yet affordable" observed the former COO at Titan Industries, Bijou Kurien. The eye gear collections were launched after an in-depth categorization of the youth segment. The City Silk sunglasses targeted the working youth in the 22-28 age group who preferred sober colors and designs. Based on the capacity of the segment to spend heavily on personal accessories, the City Silk sunglasses were launched in Rs 1495 and Rs 1995 price range. The REVV Collection was targeted at the college going youth in the 16-22 age bracket. Hence they were more stylish, brighter colored and priced between Rs 695 and Rs 1195. The sales figure in the context of FasTrack eye gears suggested that 75% of the buyers were in the 16-25 age group while the rest were in the 26-31 age bracket. With the passage of time, the FasTrack brand established itself as the third independent watch brand in the Titan stable after Sonata and the in-house brand, Titan. In this context, Bijou Kurien observed, "We had already started using FasTrack in the eye gear market, in sunglasses, where the customer is again the youth. We then decided to combine the watch and sunglasses businesses of FasTrack into a standalone brand and let it have price points as determined by the dynamics of the youth segment rather than be guided by the imperatives of the Titan brand structure."

Whirlpool:
Whirlpool, has over the years, differentiated itself from its competitors by adopting an innovative product strategy and thereby coming up with customized products for the women of today. Is has been one company that has always kept a keen eye on the lifestyle of today's women, their attitudes, tastes and preferences. One of the earliest innovations specifically addressed to the concerned segment were the smaller sized refrigerators. In various cities across the country, people stay in flats that have lots of constraints in terms of space and so smaller sized consumer durables are what they require but at the same time, they look for products that can offer more flexibility. With this feedback, Whirlpool introduced the Flexigerator that was a refrigerator with adjustable and 'drop-down' shelves. The feature offered a number of space options to customers. Whirlpool introduced shelves that could take 1.5 litre bottles, on specifically strengthened doors. It also offered superlative qualities of direct cool and frost free refrigerators that offered express cooling and in which ice could be prepared in a matter of minutes.

Whirlpool showed its sensitivity to the requirements of today's women in the context of washing machines too. It was the first to launch a Combimatic washing machine in India. It was a single tub semi-automatic washing machine that did away with the hassle of shifting clothes from one tub to another. It pioneered the unique 6th Sense technology for optimum water, detergent and temperature levels based on wash load. To relieve today's women from the hassles of hand washing clothes, Whirlpool launched the Stainwash technology. It brought together the unique properties of Hotwash and 1-2, 1-2 hand wash to completely remove common house stains. Whirlpool also introduced an exclusive agitator system in its washing machines that took care of suitable washing of large and heavy household items like curtains, table cloths etc.

In the context of brand promotion, Whirlpool, created its market position around the tagline, 'You and Whirlpool – the world's best homemakers'. The tagline encouraged and enabled today's women to consciously identify themselves as the real homemakers. Some other memorable taglines from Whirlpool have been 'Ice Ice Baby' for refrigerators and 'Mummy ka magic chalega kya?' for washing machines. The campaigns have over the years maintained a constant focus on the target audience and have been able to successfully appeal to their needs and wants. The brand's communication strategy has evolved in a nuanced manner to stay in touch with the evolution of the desires and aspirations of the homemaker, in the context of a fast changing society. Whirlpool has been successful in identifying and associating with both the women of the house as well as with women who balance domestic responsibilities with a professional career. Lately, the brand has been found to be endorsed by film stars Kajol and Ajay Devgan .

It has been widely felt to add more relevance to the promotion of the brand as has been cited by Arvind Mediratta, former vicepresident (Marketing) at Whirlpool, "First, they are a couple off screen as well, which lends credibility to the promise of partnership in homemaking. Second, they are one celebrity couple that has not been exposed on the small screen at all and thus their endorsing a brand will infuse freshness and break through the clutter in the current advertising scenario."

The brand recorded a 25% jump in gross sales in 2005 and in 2006, it was expected to capture 26% market share in the refrigerator category and 16% in the washing machine category. Commenting on the achieved and projected growth of the brand, Arvind Uppal, MD, Whirlpool India said, "Our core strength lies in the understanding of the Indian homemaker and innovating our products as per her needs and unmet desires. All the products launched here today are a result of the same exhaustive consumer insights process that we have used over the years to understand her better. We are confident that our enhanced product portfolio across categories, innovative marketing coupled with faster response to the market will be the key drivers in growing the brand to a leadership status in the Indian market."

Pantaloons:
Pantaloon Retail (India) Limited, which started as a garment retailer in 1997, has in recent times been found to focus on the youth in a big way. It has changed its positioning from a family-oriented store to a fashion store. Pantaloons, which advertised with the tagline- 'India's family store' has been found to identify the importance and potential of attracting the youth to its stores. Sanjeev Agrawal, president (Marketing) at Pantaloons observed in this context, "Looking at the demographics, India is a young country compared to the others and we wanted our brand to get associated with this emerging target audience. This is the first time that we are relaunching our stores targeting youth and even women, since they are the ones defining most purchasing decisions." Pantaloons chain of stores has undergone changes with respect to its logo, brand communication, physical layout, merchandise and mindset. The stores have been redesigned to give a feeling of "fresh feeling, fresh attitude and fresh fashion". It was done with the objective of making young people step into the Pantaloons stores and be a part of the evolving brand.

Pantaloons changed its tagline to 'Fresh Fashion' to lay more emphasis on the youth and make them an integral part of its growth strategy. Fashion is all about now. As per Agrawal, Pantaloons intended to change fashions every 4-6 weeks. People should see a fresh look every time they walk into a Pantaloons outlet. That was the thought behind the coining of the tagline. It was an idea that was effective in capturing the imagination of young India. With the focus on today's youth, Pantaloons is offering trendy and hip fashion that defines the hopes and aspirations of this demographic profile. To focus of fast changing fashion, the retail chain has tilted the balance of its merchandise in favor of in-house brands like UMM, Rig, Lombard, Bare and Denim. Besides this, Pantaloons has also been in the process of building in-store branded sections for categories like sunglasses, watches and high fashion garments to keep pace with the changing fashion trend and offer the youth the best in terms of style and looks.

To bolster the 'fresh fashion' image, Pantaloons signed Bollywood stars, Bipasha Basu and Zayed Khan to endorse the entire range of apparels like casual wear, formal wear, western wear, ethnic wear, party wear and sports wear [Exhibit VI]. It was felt that Bipasha Basu and Zayed Khan, with their distinctive style statement, would reiterate the Pantaloons' repositioning. Sanjeev Agrawal cited in this context, "Bipasha Basu and Zayed Khan will add their personal style statement to Pantaloons, which will help enhance the fashion imagery of the brand. Hence, we are proud to simultaneously sign the two Bollywood icons to endorse our flagship fashion retail brand." Bipasha Basu while expressing her satisfaction over associating with Pantaloons said, "Pantaloons has a wide range of fashion wear for women and it's this drive to continually provide 'Fresh fashion' that makes Pantaloons my store. It is a store that has fashion for all occasions."

In order to reinforce its youthful image, Pantaloons has associated with the Femina Miss India pageant of 2007. It has replaced Pond's as the title sponsor and so this year's pageant is being referred to as Pantaloons Femina Miss India 2007. Brand Pantaloons witnessed a 157% increase in net profits for the quarter ended December 31st 2006. Though various brands in India are increasingly focusing on the urban youth by designing their product and strategy mix attuned to their lifestyles and attitudes, they have so far made very little attempt to reach out to the rural youth.

Though there have been instances of 'youth' brands like Pepsi, Coke and mouth fresheners like Chlor Mint and Mint o Fresh featuring rural settings and rural youth in some of their campaigns, overall, such efforts have lacked consistency. Though the Tier 4 of the economic pyramid doesn't allow the marketers to pursue margins but they hold enough zing for the marketers in terms of volume and capital efficiency. The youth-centric marketers need to radically rethink about strategies to effectively explore the potential offered by the youth at the bottom of the economic pyramid as that can prove to be an ideal source for their long-term sustainability. The brands need to create buying power, shape aspirations, improve access and tailor local solutions if they are sincerely interested in seeking greater profits. They need to redesign their product/service mix along with their branding strategies such that they make themselves equally relevant to both the urban as well as the rural youth.

There have been success stories in the Indian market where a brand has been at the forefront to understand the needs and wants of the youth. They have offered innovative solutions and designed relevant and appealing branding strategies in their language and then there have been brands that have continued with their decade old style of working and simply trying to transplant strategies that have worked in other countries. The youth market is the hottest proposition for the Indian marketers and so they need to make that connection with the segment through relevant communication strategies. Unless India Inc. make a more sincere effort of understanding and identifying with the youth, it's quite unlikely that the youth will listen to them.

References:
Jayashankar Priyanka, "In Pursuit of Youth", The Hindu Business Line, September 9th

2004

Businessworld, Issue Dated: November 6th 2006

Kurian Boby, "Titan gets on the FasTrack", The Hindu Business Line, July 28th 2005

Lakshman Nandini, "Wooing Generation Next",
http://www.rediff.com/money/2004/jun/12spec.htm, June 12th 2004

Chatterjee Purvita, "Pantaloon relaunches stores targeting youth", The Hindu Business Line, October 4th 2005

Celebrity Endorsements: How They Shaped Brand Bikini's Identity?

Bikini (from the Latin bi, meaning "two", and kini, meaning "square inches of Lycra"), the world's most controversial attire for women turned sixty in the year 2006. "It has weathered scandal, shrugged off the fads and whims of fashion, been celebrated as helping with the emancipation of women and lambasted as turning women into objects of desire. Its wearers have passed into legend, becoming iconic images of 20th Century culture."

Bikini as an attire for women was initially shunned as it was felt that it turned women into desirable commodities and was a threat to any civilized society. However, celebrity endorsements since the 1950s have ensured not just the acceptability of the two- piece but also its evolution into more daring avatars over the years. The bikini that started as a brand name* in 1946 (when it was introduced by Louis Reard, a French automotive engineer) has over the years become a generic name for the product category called swimsuits. Through aggressive endorsements of the bikini on a global scale, celebrities from the world of fashion and entertainment have been found to offer a distinct identity to the attire and have turned it into a costume that is sure to trigger some kind of involuntary reaction within any onlooker.

There are six facets of any brand's identity as suggested by Jean-Noel Kapferer viz. physical facet, personality, culture, consumer mentalisation, reflected consumer and relationship. Among these, there are facets that are internal to a brand like its personality, culture and consumer mentalisation while there are some facets that are external to a brand like its physical facet, its relationship with the society and the reflected consumer characteristics. In the case of bikini; it was found that these got a more definite meaning through celebrity endorsements .

Brand Bikini: The Physical Facet

The bikini was a type of women's bathing suit, characterized by two separate parts- one covering the breasts, the other the groin (and optionally the buttocks), leaving an uncovered area between the two parts of the garment. Right from the 1950s, bikini has been observed to be endorsed by those beauties who possessed an enviably supple physique. Hollywood actresses like Ursula Andress and Raquel Welch turned the bikini into iconic bathing attire for women when they donned it in movies like Dr. No and One Million Years B.C (**Exhibit-I**). Their supple and athletic physique imparted such a tempting and enviable physical facet to the bikini that young ladies across the globe made genuine efforts to secure a physique for themselves that allowed them to wear the bikini and show off their bodies.

Exhibit-I
Bikini Girls: Ursula Andress and Raquel Welch

The introduction of swimsuit rounds in International beauty pageants like the Miss Universe and Miss World was another trigger for young women to crave for the bikini and adopt it whole-heartedly. In such pageants, beautiful ladies with enviable physical attributes donned the bikini and walked the ramp that reinforced the sleek and sexy physical quality of the bikini (**Exhibit-II**)

Exhibit-II
Bikini in Beauty Pageants

In the Indian context, where actors and actresses of Bollywood introduce new fashion trends, bikini was observed to be worn by actresses like Zeenat Aman, Parveen Babi and Dimple Kapadia who were not just beautiful but possessed simply 'irresistible' physique. In recent times, actresses like Bipasha Basu and Deepika Padukone have been often found to don the bikini which again proves how celebrities with great physique have made bikini eternally sensual and lovable bathing attire through endorsements (**Exhibit-III**).

Exhibit-III
Bollywood Actresses Donning the Bikini

The Personality Facet of Bikini

Apart from the physical facet, the personality facet too has been shaped by celebrities over the decades. The Bond Girls in the James Bond movies have been consistently found to don the two-piece. Right from Ursula Andress in Dr. No to Halle Berry in Die Another Day, Bond Girls with their perfectly toned bodies, sensational and seductive personality have influenced the personality facet of Brand Bikini. The Bond Girls were at times also found to portray daring characters in movies just as were the star cast of the television series, Baywatch. Baywatch highlighted a team of male and female lifeguards who were ever ready to risk their lives to save people from drowning in the sea (Exhibit-IV). The daring persona along with sensual personality thus became the hallmark of the personality facet of bikini.

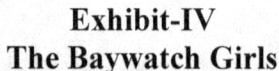

Exhibit-IV
The Baywatch Girls

Celebrities and Bikini's Cultural Facet

Bikini has always been understood as a symbol of women's emancipation. The very invention of the two-piece was to offer a feeling of liberty to women. Reard had observed that the Parisian women liked to roll down their tops and bottoms of their two-pieces for better tan while they were on the beaches and this prompted him to design the skimpy bathing attire. Whether it were the Hollywood actresses donning the bikini or the actresses in Bollywood, the basic objective of wearing the bikini was to openly showcase women's liberation. Even the introduction of swimsuit rounds in beauty pageants was a step in that context. Women's liberalization was the core element that served as a fodder for the brand's inspiration.

Brand Bikini and Consumer Mentalisation

Bikini has been found to have a rebellious and carefree attitude and mentality. This has been shaped over the years due to the personalities who have endorsed it. When the bikini was introduced to the world, women from conservative family background shunned it since the attire exposed the navel which was considered indecent at that point of time. There was no one to model for the attire and finally it was Micheline Bernardini, a nude bar dancer who agreed to model for the two-piece **(Exhibit-V)**. A nude bar dancer as such is supposed to have both a rebellious and carefree attitude since no one at least in the 1940s, took up that profession out of choice but was forced by the society in some way or the other to take up such a profession. Once, the initial inhibition is shed, people belonging to such a profession become carefree about exposing themselves in public view. Thus this initial endorsement was the seed for the shaping of brand bikini's attitude and mentality.

Exhibit-V
Micheline Bernardini Endorsing Bikini

In the later years, Hollywood actresses in Bond movies and Bollywood actresses like Zeenat Aman and Parveen Babi were all personalities who possessed a rebellious character and hardly cared about exposing in public. They were confident of their physique and were convinced that it was cool to wear the revealing outfit.

The Reflected Consumer Facet

The consumers or users of bikini had been found to be personalities who were experimental and believed in setting trends. Initially, bikini was not allowed to seek entry into American popular culture. But then, when movie stars like Marilyn Monroe, Rita Hayworth and Elizabeth Taylor adopted the bikini as a beach wear, people started embracing it (Exhibit-VI). In India, when movies showcased conservative story plots and traditionally dressed actresses, Sharmila Tagore was found to don the bikini in the movie, An Evening in Paris. Tagore thus proved that she was experimental in dressing herself with something that she felt comfortable in and took pride in being a trendsetter. Princess Diana, who belonged to the royal family of Buckingham Palace, donned the bikini which was another example of the experimental and trendsetting character of bikini's consumers.

Exhibit-VI
Hayworth, Taylor and Monroe: The Trendsetters in Hollywood

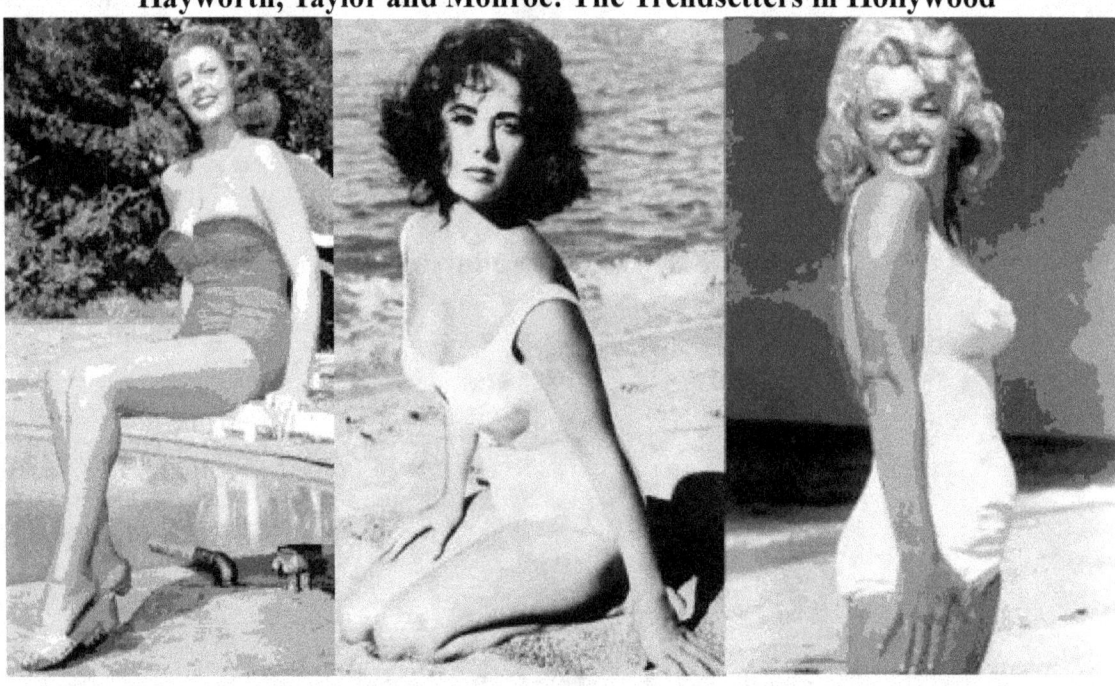

Bikini: It's Relationship with the Society
The bikini's relationship with the society across the globe had been found to be controversial over the years. The society held contradictory viewpoints. A section of the society was found to be quite positive about the growing popularity of the two-piece. They held the view that it was the bikini that heralded the message of women's emancipation across the globe. The bikini enabled the women to express and communicate themselves in a better way. On the other hand, another section of the society held the view that the bikini actually gave birth to the concept of commoditization of women's bodies. It projected women in a bad way and indirectly made them victims of sexual assault. It was this perennial debate within the society since bikini's introduction that sustained the popularity of the two-piece. Often, wearing the bikini made a celebrity controversial. When Sharmila Tagore donned the bikini in the 1960s, many eye brows were raised and she was criticized for her bold move. Controversies surrounded models from predominantly Muslim countries like Afghanistan and Indonesia when they walked the ramp in a bikini at various beauty pageants. The examples cited above clearly indicate that celebrities endorsing the bikini have been largely responsible in shaping its identity. The identity has been durable for decades and highly explicit vis-à-vis other forms of women's attire.

Brand Identity Prism for Brand Bikini

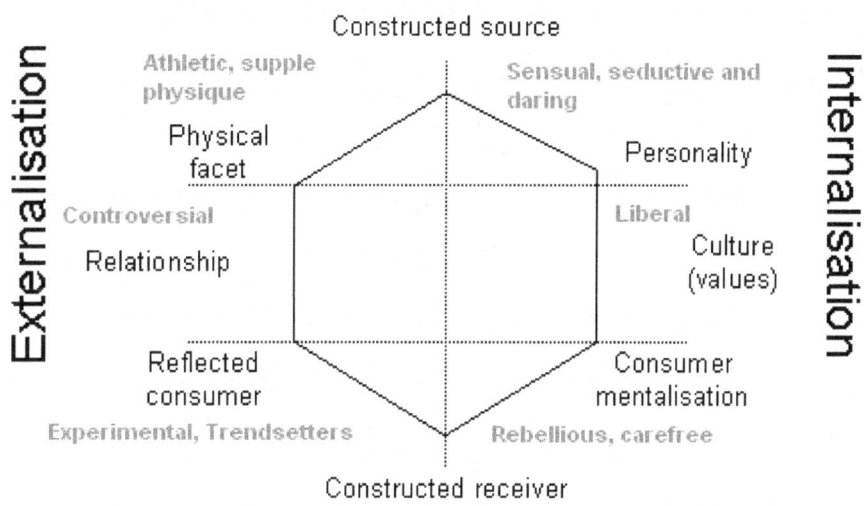

References:

Westcott Kathryn, "The bikini: Not a brief affair", **h**ttp://news.bbc.co.uk/go/pr/fr/-/2/hi/in_depth/5130460.stm,
July 5th 2006

http://en.wikipedia.org/wiki/Bikini

Rubin Sylvia, "Fashion shocker of '46: the naked belly button But the bikini wasn't a hit until Sixties", http://www.sfgate.com/cgi-bin/article.cgi?file=/c/a/2006/07/02/MNGOQJO6OK1.DTL, July 2nd 2006

Sage Adam, Bikini turns 60, barely enough for a brief history
http://www.theaustralian.news.com.au/story/0,20876,18818136-2703,00.html, April 15th 2006

Kapferer Noel-Jean, Strategic Brand Management, 2nd Edition

Brand Lux and Movie Stars: The Cinematic Connection

Lux, a brand synonymous with beauty worldwide was launched in India in 1929. In 1934, the first Lux bar was made in India which sold for a princely sum of two annas. Since its launch in India, Lux offered a range of soaps in different colors and fragrances. However, each variant of the brand was found to offer the same benefit and that was the benefit of beautiful skin. The unique and desirable fragrances along with nourishing ingredients made bathing with Lux a pleasurable experience for the Indian consumers.

Over the years, Lux has been found to retain its leadership status in its product category by vividly differentiating itself from competing brands. There has been no soap brand that could create as much aspirational value as Lux. The aspirations were built around the punchline – 'the beauty soap of film stars'. Various gorgeous faces from Bollywood have come out in the open from time to time with their beauty secret, Lux while endorsing the brand. The very first matinee idol who endorsed the brand was Leela Chitnis [**Exhibit-I**].

Exhibit-I
Leela Chitnis Endorsing Lux

It has been due to the strong, durable and desirable brand values [**Exhibit-II**] that Lux has not just maintained its leadership status for decades but has also set benchmarks for competition.

Exhibit-II
The Brand Values of Lux

Brand Values
_ Lux is truly an international brand that believes in beauty and has always celebrated it.
_ Lux beauty is glamorous, sophisticated and luxurious.
_ Lux believes in a woman taking pleasure in herself, for herself. But, however, much Lux might

indulge the user with its pleasures, it never makes her feel guilty. Lux has always legitimised beauty for women.

_ Lux does not hold a mirror up to its consumers. It shows the way. It tells stories about the consumer realising her most beautiful, ideal self. It recognises that wanting to look and feel beautiful is one of the most fundamental human motivations there is.

_ Lux believes that beauty should not be hidden. Lux does not subscribe to the philosophy that says beauty comes only from the inside. However, Lux is not shallow or lacking in any substance. Lux knows better than any other brand the meaning and importance of beauty for women. Lux knows that when a woman feels she looks beautiful, her true character and individuality are liberated and are able to shine through – whether it's gaining the respect and admiration of others, or connecting with the world on one's own terms.

Lux has been the most desired brand for generations as it offered an experience of sensuous and luxurious bathing. Lux campaigns have wooed millions of people over the years. It has been an intimate partner of some of the most dazzling stars of the silver screen. Brand Lux has saluted their impeccable beauty, has heralded their stardom and has promised their beauty and complexion to ordinary women. The brand has been endorsed by more than 50 film stars of the Indian film industry. From Madhubala to Madhuri, from Babita to Karishma and Kareena, from Raveena to Rani, each have endorsed the goodness of bathing with Lux and the feeling of luxury and self-pampering associated with it. It is thus natural that the brand has over a period of time built equity and has been referred as the best beauty soap in India. By using a leading film star in the advertisements, Brand Lux has fulfilled consumer's aspirations of using beauty soaps based on the rationale, 'if it's good enough for a film star, it's good for me'. Later, this idea moved into a transformational role where bathing with Lux transported the user into a land of fantasy.

Lux as a brand has always been successful in its attempt to convey a youthful and contemporary image. Since the early 1990s, Lux was found to associate with those actresses of Bollywood who received the best debutant award at the Filmfare Awards. The awards category was aptly called Lux Face of the Year. Raveena Tandon, Mahima Chaudhary, Rani Mukherjee, Aishwarya Rai and Kareena Kapoor have been the various Bollywood actresses who received this award and were later found to endorse the brand in various advertisements.

Lux has been found to evolve with the changing needs of consumers in India. In the late 1980s, a new consumer set emerged who had sophisticated beauty and bathing needs. Lux identified the emergence of a premium segment in the soap category and so in 1989, a range of premium soaps were launched to suit the evolving needs of the consumers. Lux started catering to two market segments viz. the popular and the premium category. Lux Toilet Soap catered to the popular segment. The range of soaps in the popular category were enriched with the goodness of a variety of nourishing ingredients like rose extracts, almond oil, milk cream, fruit extracts and honey.

The premium category had International Lux that had a range of moisturizing, deep cleansing and sunscreen soaps. The packaging of the soaps in the two categories was attuned to the aspirational levels of the consumers. In the early 2000s, Lux in an attempt to make the rural consumers experience pleasurable bathing launched Mini Lux that was priced at Rs. 5 only. The strategy brought Lux within the reach of 300 million rural consumers. With the introduction of new perfume and ingredient variants, Mini Lux proved instrumental in increasing the market share of the brand by 4% between 2003 and 2005.

In 2003, Lux Toilet Soap was re-launched to offer better product quality vis-à-vis other competing brands in its category. In order to establish the presence of nourishing ingredients in the re-launched Lux, a unique concept, 'ingredients you can see in the soap' was coined. A novel metallic substrate packaging highlighted the ingredients in the soap and the ingredient-linked perfumes enhanced the sensorial experience. Each of the variants in the relaunched soap range had milk cream with the active ingredients of rose extracts, sandal saffron, almond oil and fruit extracts .

However, it was found that the communication strategy associated with the brand was gradually loosing its relevance as consumers started doubting that whether the brand was really being used by film stars. In addition to this, se veral competing beauty soap brands had adopted a similar advertising strategy where the brand was being endorsed by a Bollywood actress. For example, Nirma Beauty Soap was being endorsed by Sonali Bendre and Nima Sandal Gold was being endorsed by Preeti Jhangiani.

With the objective of countering the decline in the brand's market share, a new communication strategy was devised. The strategy of bringing out the star in an individual was found to make the brand move away from the long-running film star route. The film stars continued to feature in the advertisements but not as her gorgeous self but rather as an alter ego or projection of the protagonist (who was an ordinary girl). Moreover the time period for which the celebrity was shown in the ad was limited to just a few seconds. By moving away from a film star and her fantasy world and focusing on an ordinary girl's star quality, Lux was found to make a distinct shift in the norms that it had set in its advertising over the years. In the new communication strategy, the film star (Aishwarya Rai) was there as a communication device to highlight the star quality in every Lux user. The punch line associated with the advertisements, 'Mujh mein star jagaye' was found to put the consumer at the heart of the brand's promise. The promise went beyond the functional benefits and the bathing luxury associated with Brand Lux. The message that the new Lux campaign communicated was that with Lux on her side, an ordinary woman can impact the world around her with her own star quality. Commenting on the strategy, Gopal Vittal, former VP (Personal Wash) at HLL said, "We have been making fairly significant changes in the marketing and advertising for the brand. Earlier the brand was just endorsed by film stars but now there is a greater degree of relevance to show the aspirational appeal. In the advertising we have taken creative licence to show the feelings of a normal girl and her aspirations to become a star."

There were several promotional campaigns that were designed around the new strategy. One such campaign was the 'Lux Star Bano, Aish Karo' contest launched in 2004. As per the campaign Lux consumers needed to buy a promotional pack of Lux soap that came with a scratch card. The 50 lucky winners were to be flown to Mumbai along with their spouses to live a day like Aishwarya Rai would. Along with gift vouchers, the winners were offered a dinner date with the former Miss World. Expressing his views regarding the promotion campaign, Vittal opined, "This promotion aims to drive the brand proposition — Mujh mein star jagaye — further. The Lux `Be a Star' promotion is an unique offering which offers consumers an opportunity to experience the life of Aishwarya Rai, and bring the proposition to life."

In 2005, Brand Lux turned 75 years. To commemorate the achievement, HLL, the company behind Lux along with the advertising agency, JWT, chose Shah Rukh Khan to endorse the brand. Brand Lux that had a strong feminine face and appeal suddenly had a male face to endorse it. In its 75th year, HLL wanted to do something really different for the brand and were interested in going for an 'out-of-box' solution. Ashok Venkatramani, VP (Skin Care) at HLL while explaining the reasons for choosing SRK said, "Shah Rukh is a big draw and women just love him. Putting the two together, we thought we could reach our consumers with the new campaign." Nandita Chalam, Associate VP and Senior Creative Director at JWT opined, "The target audience for Lux is women. Shah Rukh is a great favourite with women of all ages. So the strategy for Lux has not really changed. It is just the execution that is very different; instead of a female star in the tub, we have Shah Rukh." The campaign featured SRK immersed in a bath tub with petals and talking about 'his beauty secrets' ('Meri Sundarta Ka Raaz') while there were four actresses (Hema Malini, Sridevi, Juhi Chawla and Kareena Kapoor) surrounding him who represented a particular decade when she had been considered an icon of beauty. Commenting on the commercial, M.G. Parameswaran, Executive Director at FCB Ulka Advertising observed, "Lux is using SRK for ostensibly a special occasion of 75 years. And apparently it has used male stars in the past in international markets. So while it is a big departure, it is with a reason. And the ad is not claiming that SRK is using the brand. He is not shown using the soap. He is merely in a bath tub surrounded by the Lux stars. So it is a device to inject a bit of novelty and `buzz value' into an old brand."

To add more zing to the celebration, HLL launched a promotional campaign named 'Har Star Lucky Star'. All wrappers of Lux had a star printed inside them. As per the terms and conditions of the campaign if the consumer found written inside the star, any number from 1 to 5, she would get an equivalent discount (in rupees) on her purchase from her shopkeeper. If the consumer found "75 years" written inside the star, she would get a year's supply of Lux free. In 2007, Lux Pink has been launched in a 'Special Edition' pack. The new variant called Lux Haute Pink has a new color and fragrance. The packaging is quite distinct in comparison with other variants of the brand .

The message behind the commercial that showcases the new variant is 'Beauty is not a color or a fragrance...its an attitude! Lux invites you to wear this attitude everyday, to enter a world where we celebrate the pleasures of beauty. Lux. Play with beauty.' The television campaign shows Aishwarya Rai for a few seconds in the initial moments of the commercial and then it zooms on various ordinary ladies who are found to take a very close look at their facial beauty. The punch line of the commercial is 'Surat bhi Hai. Khubsurat bhi Hai.' In short, the campaign is the continuation of the communication strategy that the brand has adopted for quite some time now.

The consistent repositioning in the brand's product development as well as communication strategy over the years have been the key factors behind the sustainable leadership of Brand Lux. Its value share as of 2007 is 17.9%. Three in every five Indian consumers has been found to enjoy the luxurious bathing pleasure of Lux during the course of a year. It has been this strong association with consumers that has made Lux one of the most trusted heritage brands of India. Lux as a brand continues to shine and captivate millions even after 75 years of existence.

References:
http://www.superbrandsindia.com/superbrands2003/lux/lux.htm
http://www.thehindubusinessline.com/catalyst/2005/09/29/
stories/2005092900160300.htm
marketingpractice.blogspot.com/2007/01/lux-celebrating-beauty.html

DISSERTATION – I

CELEBRITY ENDORSEMENTS ON TELEVISION AND ITS IMPACT ON BRANDS

By Poulami Roy under the guidance of Prof. Kisholoy Roy

Abstract

Celebrity endorsement has nowadays become a pervasive element in advertising and communication management. India as a country is known for loving its stars. The Indians idolize their Bollywood actors and cricketers. The advertisers see this as an opportunity to grab and work on so as to expand their operations and promote their product. For this reason we generally find that a particular celebrity who is popular among the mass is used not by just one company but by various endorsers to cater to a larger market. The basic assumption underlying celebrity endorsement is that the value associated with the celebrity is transferred to the brand and therefore it helps in creating an image that can be easily referred by consumers. As a result, the brand can very quickly establish the credibility and thus can get immediate identification and in a manner can improve sales.

With this idea as a backdrop a field study was conducted with the objective to analyze the present scenario of celebrity campaigns in India and the impact that they create on the minds of people, to understand how multiple endorsements by celebrities (sportsperson or movie stars) have paved its way as a form of communication by different firms successfully, to the extent of relatedness of celebrity endorsements with that of consumer purchase behavior, analyze at which stage a brand needs endorsement by different celebrity in the entire life cycle of the brand, understand the impact that a controversial celebrity creates when they endorse any brand and to analyze whether there exists any correlation between the age of an endorser and the average age of the target audience.

Introduction

Celebrities are people who enjoy public recognition by a large share of a certain group people whereas attributes like attractiveness, extraordinary lifestyle are just examples and specific common characteristics cannot be observed though it can be said that within a corresponding social group celebrities generally differ from the social norm and enjoy a high degree of public awareness. Celebrities are popular among the public and they take pleasure in being recognized by numerous people. Good looks, classy lifestyles and special skills are only some of celebrities' special features that are different from general people and are seen by the public, which grants them a large amount of the public's attention. It explains that a celebrity is a person such as an actor, sportsman, entertainer, etc, who is different from the general public and is recognized by them because of his or her achievements. One of the methods that firms use for their brand communication is endorsement. In this method they use celebrities to play the role of the spokesperson for their brand, which assures their brand's place within the society by promoting the celebrity's personality, fame and their influence on the public's decisions. Celebrity endorsement can play a vital leading role when it comes to leading the public's decisions, in a market which has a vast number of local, regional, and international brands. In recent years, using celebrity endorsers has become more common.

Making use of celebrities as part of a firms marketing strategy is a popular way of supporting the image of a firm's brand. Large amounts of money are spent by companies, only to create brands which hold three important characteristics which are given by their celebrity endorsers: likeability, attractiveness and trustworthiness. Firms must form their brands with celebrity endorsers that include sportsmen and movie stars, hoping that the celebrities can create more successful and impressionable marketing and corporate communications, which will earn the firm more profit.In today's world, to support their corporate or brand image, it is conventional for major firms to use celebrity endorsers in their marketing communications strategy. An important concern is to find out how many celebrities really consume the products that they endorse. In addition, another important issue is that marketers sometimes endorse products that are unhealthy for us and the environment. Our purpose is to unveil and introduce a new the positive effects that celebrity endorsement has on a brand's image and to discover the most important factors that an effective endorsement relies on. Firms aim to influence the behavior of consumers by using celebrity endorsers, so that they will be tempted to buy their products. To discover the customers' response towards the product and brand image that celebrities are endorsing, four questions will be analyzed in this research.

At present celebrity voice-overs in advertising is an emerging trend noticed in India. Some celebrities have distinct voices which are recognizable even when they not present on-screen. Mr. Amitabh Bachchan in Indian context is one such example. This is a more subtle way to add celebrity branding to a product or service. In India, Celebrity endorsement started gaining prominence since 1980's. The introduction of television added a variable effective medium of communication. Celebrities are people who are recognized by a large group of people. Celebrities may convey a broad range of meanings, involving demographic, personality and lifestyle types. One of the primary goals of advertising is the persuasion of customers, i.e., the active attempt to change or modify consumer's attitude towards brands. In this respect, the credibility of an advertisement plays an important role in convincing the target audience of the attractiveness of the company's brand. Pursuing a celebrity endorsement strategy enables advertisers to project a credible image in terms of expertise, persuasiveness, trustworthiness, and objectiveness.

Marketers have been leveraging on celebrity appeal for a long time. One can still remember brands like Vimal, Thums-Up, Gwalior and Dinesh Suiting using star-appeal in the early days of mass advertising. There was a burst of advertisements, featuring stars like Tabassum (Prestige Pressure-cooker), Jalal Agha (Pan Parag Pan-masaala). This remembrance or recall factor is true not only for classic forms of celebrities like actors (ex Sharukh khan, Amitabh Bachhan), models (John Abraham, Malaika Arora, Diya Mirza) Sports athletes (ex. Sachin Tendulkar, Sania Mirza), entertainers (Shekhar Suman) and pop Stars (Mika, Daler Mehndi) but also for less obvious groups like businessmen (ex Dirubhai Ambani) or politicians (Laloo Prasad Yadav) but also for fictional celebrities like Ronald McDonald, Fido dido, gattu, Amul Girl, Pillsbury doughboy and others. Celebrities appear in public in different ways. First, they appear in public when fulfilling their profession ex Sachin Tendulkar is loved by millions for his wonderful performance in the cricket fields. Furthermore, celebrities appear in public by attending special celebrity events ex. filmfare star awards, Videocon screen awards etc. In addition they are present in News, Fashion magazines and tabloids, which provide second source of information on events and private life of celebrities through mass media channels. The dawn of the 21st century saw the phenomenon of celebrity endorsement gaining prominence in our country. Multinationals as well as domestic companies are going the extra yard to sign up leading Hindi Film stars for endorsing their brands. In recent times, we had the Shah Rukh- Santro campaign with the objective of overcoming the hindrance that an unknown Korean company (Hyundai Motors) faced in the Indian market. The objective was to earn faster brand recognition, association and emotional unity with the target group.

The below mentioned two approaches helps to explain the topic concerned in more detailed manner:

The Match-up Hypothesis
Literature reveals that a spokesperson interacts with the type of brand being advertised. According to Friedman and Friedman (1979), a famous relative to a 'normal' spokesperson is more effective for products high in psychological or social risk, involving such elements as good taste, self-image, and opinion of others. Several research studies have examined the congruency between celebrity endorsers and brands to explain the effectiveness of using famous persons to promote brands. Results show that a number of celebrity endorsements proved very successful, whereas others completely failed, resulting in the 'termination' of the respective celebrity communicator.

The Meaning Transfer Model
McCracken (1989) has explained the effectiveness of celebrity spokespersons by assessing the meanings consumers associate with the endorser and eventually transfer to the brand. This perspective was shared by Kambitsis et al. (2002, p. 160), who found the athletes' personality as being an important factor in influencing "specific target groups, to which such personalities are easily recognizable and much admired." McCracken has suggested a meaning transfer model that is composed of three subsequent stages. First, the meaning associated with the famous person moves from the endorser to the product or brand. Thus, meanings attributed to the celebrity become associated with the brand in the consumer's mind. Finally, in the consumption process, the brand's meaning is acquired by the

customer. The third stage of the model explicitly shows the importance of the consumer's role in the process of endorsing brands with famous persons. The meaning transfer process is shown in the figure below:

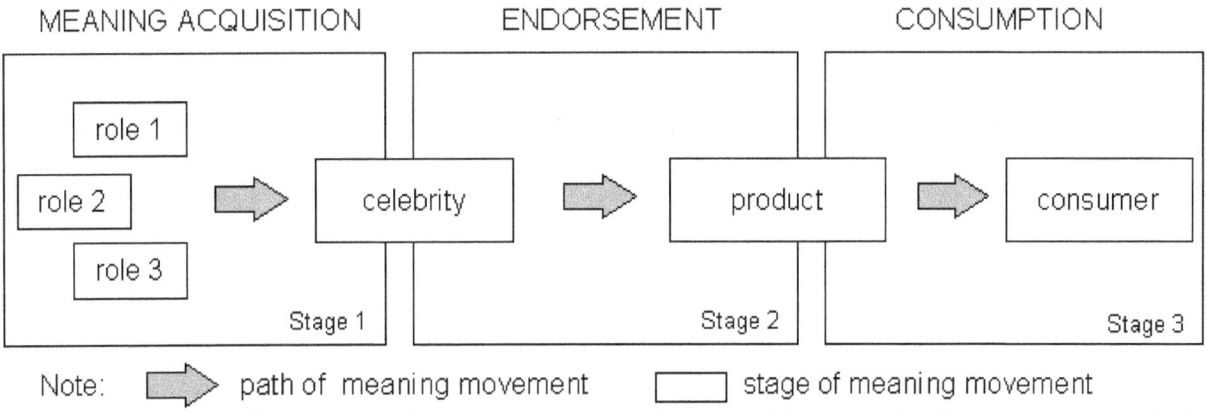

Figure: Meaning transfer in the endorsement process (Adapted from McCracken 1989)

With celebrity spokespersons representing a diverse mix of type, gender, and age, they can effectively be used to endorse specific brand lines of a company as shown by the cosmetic manufacturer L'Oreal, which matches its diverse product lines in accordance with the celebrity's meanings. The watch manufacturer Omega, for example, promotes its brand by matching selected celebrities with the company's product lines.

Literature Review

Celebrity Endorsement is a way of communicating the idea of any product from the manufacturer's end to the customer by using the image of a personality or an endorser (Agrawal and Dubey, 2012). The people of our society desire to own the products which are the most suitable to their persona. The people are always in search of right things which suits to their personality, whether it is a cell phone, a mobile network, apparels and the list goes on. They are of the belief that if a particular celebrity of their choice or liking has endorsed a particular product or appears in the advertisement, then the product will be also right for them. The presence of the choice of celebrity plays a huge role here. People generally tend to buy those products which their favorite personality has endorsed. Successful branding programs are initiated for the same purpose. The message that the company tries to convey through these programs is that there is no other product like their product in the market, in a way they show that customers have just their product as the best option and thus compels the customers to buy that particular product.

In today's world companies are investing more and more on celebrities to promote not only their product but also their brand (Sonwalkar et al,2011). As the use of celebrities is increasing so is the case of the impact that it creates on the minds of the consumers. So the impact that different celebrities creates is not always positive but at the same time overshadowing of the products can also be seen. At the same time it can be seen that for certain products or brands controversies are created in the market which can hamper the image of a brand. In many cases it can be seen that liking for a certain product can be created but the loyalty towards a certain brand is shaken. The influence that it has definitely gives a remembrance factor for the mass.

At present celebrity endorsement is a buzz word all over the world and it the situation is not different in India (Patra and Datta, 2010) The use of Integrated Marketing Communication has played a huge role in bringing the desired message required for targeting the mass. The emergence of celebrity endorsement in India started with the coming of globalization, the need for celebrities who are accepted among the masses created the buzz for different products. The use of suitable celebrity for a particular brand and product type is what the concerned is for all companies. The emerging trends and challenges have compelled companies to think of the endorser whether it is a sports personality or a movie star who will be accepted by the people for a particular product category. The trend and lifestyle of people are changing rapidly with the changing times so is the advertisements and the endorsers. Hence the concept of Integrated Marketing Communication has paved its way for the companies to connect to a larger target audience base.

The use of superstars in advertising generates a lot of publicity and attention from the public (Schlecht, 2003). Companies generally promote their brands using superstars and they consequently generate higher revenues for themselves. The question arises here is just that whether to rely on those superstars or the brands or we can say that whether the source is credible or not. The relationship between the celebrity endorsements and brands creates a positive impact not only among the consumers but also brings positive result for the company. Celebrities act as a spokesperson for the brands and thus generate positive word of mouth for a particular brand or a product.

The use of heartthrob celebrities helps to cover some part of the cost that has been incurred by the company (Sindhu, 2011). The use of certain male celebrities in case of certain products is much more acceptable than when endorsed by female celebrities. The use of celebrities in some cases gives results which only brings "feel good" factor for brands and not actually increase sales. Presence of celebrities just increases the appeal of the company and not actually brings in sales. Consumers generally get tempted to follow a particular brand or an advertisement due to the presence of his favorite personality. For the big brands, they generally target the customer to impress them by the use of such personalities who are famous in their respective fields and have maximum likability among the mass.

Research Objective

- To understand the preference for celebrity endorsement over non celebrity endorsement among the audience

- To analyze the impact of endorsements on the value of a brand and the awareness that it creates

- To analyze the extent of relatedness of celebrity endorsements with that of consumer purchase behavior

- To understand the acceptability of brands being endorsed by different celebrity endorser and which among them is the most effective

- To identify the type of endorser; rising or established celebrity which would yield greater dividend for a company

- To analyze at which stage a brand needs endorsement by different celebrity in the entire life cycle of the brand

- To analyze the effect an endorser creates when he endorses multiple brands at the same time

- To understand the impact that a controversial celebrity creates when they endorse any brand

- To analyze whether there exists any correlation between the age of an endorser and the average age of the target audience

Research Hypothesis

H1:   There is no significant difference between the gender of respondents and their preference for watching celebrity endorsement over non celebrity advertisement

H2:   There is no significant difference between the gender of respondents and their perception of the brand value getting enhanced through celebrity endorsement

H3:   There is no significant difference between the gender of respondents and their perception towards creating quicker awareness for brands by the celebrities

H4:   There is no significant difference between the gender of respondents and their perception regarding the extent of relationship between celebrity endorsements and consumer purchase behavior

H5:   There is no significant difference between the gender of respondents and their perception regarding the relative impact created by the foreign versus Indian celebrities

H6:   There is no significant difference between the gender of respondents and their perception regarding the role of controversial celebrities in brand endorsements

H7:   There is no significant difference between the gender of respondents and their opinion regarding the correlation in age of endorser and average age of target audience for a brand

H8:   There is no significant difference between the gender of respondents and their opinion regarding popular celebrities enhancing the "feel good" factor for brand

Research Methodology

40 individuals in the age bracket of 18-35 were surveyed. Majority of the respondents were students pursuing MBA program while the rest were service holders. The maximum numbers of informants were post graduate with an age limit of 18-25 years. A combination of judgmental and convenience sampling was used to select the informants for the study. A structured questionnaire was used to collect responses. Responses were sourced from the Kolkata market through personal interview method.

Research Findings

Informants were asked whether endorsements by celebrities could create quicker brand awareness. It was found that 53% of the respondents (out of 40) said 'yes', 38% said 'to a certain extent', 8% of the respondents were 'neutral' towards it and only 3% said 'no' it does not create quicker brand awareness.

They were further asked about the celebrity types which is acceptable across product categories, 23 out of 40 respondents were found that they accept movie stars across all product categories, 3 said TV stars, 7 were in favor of 'celebrities who appear both on television and in movies and only 1 was in favor of 'corporate personality'. It was further felt that the study needs to highlight among the sports personalities, which sportsperson are accepted across all product categories, they were given options like; 'cricketers', 'footballers', 'tennis players', 'badminton players' and 'others'. It was found that 93% said cricketers, 3% each for footballers, tennis and badminton players. None of them have gone for the option 'others'.

The study further helped to find out that which is the most preferred channel where the informants feel celebrity endorsements works the best. Among the options given, it was found that 23 out of 40 said 'general entertainment channels', 4 said 'music channels' 2 said 'news channel, 11 were of the opinion that 'it works well in all types of channel' and none of the respondents voted for 'sports channels'. Then the informants asked about, whether a 'brand face' or 'brand ambassador' creates more positive impact on brands, 75 % of the respondents were in favor of 'brand ambassador' and 25% said that 'brand face' would create more positive impact on brands.

Respondents were further asked that when the recall for brands gets enhanced in the context of endorsements. Of the options given, 63% (25 out of 40) said 'when celebrities appear as themselves', 23% (9 out of 40) said 'when they appear in their fictional avatars (due to a soap/movie) and 15 % (6 out of 40) favored 'when celebrities appear in a character developed for the advertisement only'. Informants were further asked about the type of celebrity which would be effective for promoting a particular brand in a particular region. The options they were given included; first 'Celebrity who is familiar and popular nationally', second 'Celebrity who is familiar and popular within a region only' and third 'Celebrity who is familiar nationally but popular within a region only'. 35 % of the respondents favored the 3rd option and 33 % each were in favor of the 1st two options.

Informants were asked during the survey that whether they prefer watching celebrity endorsement over non celebrity endorsement or not. The question was put to both the male and female respondents of the survey. A chi square test was performed based on the data obtained to find out if significant differences existed between the genders of respondents and their preference for celebrity endorsement. The p-value obtained was 0.167. Since, $p > 0.05$, **H1 which states that there is no significant difference between** the gender of respondents and their preference for watching celebrity endorsement over non celebrity advertisement stands accepted.

Informants were asked during the survey that whether brand value gets enhanced with celebrity endorsement or not. The question was put to both the male and female respondents of the survey. A chi square test was performed based on the data obtained to find out if significant differences existed between the genders of respondents and the aspect that brand value gets enhanced through celebrity endorsement. The p-value obtained was 0.663. Since, $p > 0.05$, **H2 which states that there is no significant difference between the gender of respondents and their perception of the brand value getting enhanced through celebrity endorsement stands accepted.**

Informants were asked during the survey that whether endorsement by celebrities create quicker awareness for brands. The question was put to both the male and female respondents of the survey. A chi square test was performed based on the data obtained to find out if significant differences existed between the genders of respondents and the awareness that celebrity endorsements create. 21 out of 40 respondents were of the opinion that presence of celebrities in advertisements creates quicker awareness for brands. The p-value obtained was 0.280. Since, $p > 0.05$, **H3 which states that there is no significant difference between the gender of respondents and their perception towards creating quicker awareness for brands by the celebrities stands accepted.**

Informants were asked during the survey that whether they feel that celebrity endorsement and consumer purchase behavior is related or not. The question was put to both the male and female respondents of the survey. A chi square test was performed based on the data obtained to find out if significant differences existed between the genders of respondents and their inclination towards the fact that consumer purchase behavior is related to celebrity endorsement. The p-value obtained was 0.358. Since, $p > 0.05$, **H4 which states that there is no significant difference between the gender of respondents and their perception regarding the extent of relationship between celebrity endorsements and consumer purchase behavior stands accepted.**

Informants were asked during the survey that which among foreign and Indian celebrities creates more impact among the consumers. The question was put to both the male and female respondents of the survey. A chi square test was performed based on the data obtained to find out if significant differences existed between the genders of respondents and their preference for foreign or Indian celebrity endorsement. The p-value obtained was 0.795. Since, $p>0.05$, **H5 which states that there is no significant difference between the gender of respondents and their perception regarding the relative impact created by the foreign versus Indian celebrities stands accepted.**

Informants were asked during the survey that what kind of impact controversial celebrities create on brand. The question was put to both the male and female respondents of the survey. A chi square test was performed based on the data obtained to find out if significant differences existed between the genders of respondents and what they feel about what role does controversial celebrities create on brand. The p-value obtained was 0.559. Since, $p>0.05$, **H6 which states that there is no significant difference between the gender of respondents and their perception regarding the role of controversial celebrities in brand endorsements stands accepted.**

Informants of the study were asked about whether correlation exists in age of endorser and average age of target audience. The question was put to both the male and female respondents of the survey. A chi square test was performed based on the data obtained to find out if significant differences existed between the genders of respondents and the aspect that correlation exists between the age of endorser and average age of target audience. The p-value obtained was 0.971. Since, $p>0.05$, **H7 which states that there is no significant difference between the gender of respondents and their opinion regarding the correlation in age of endorser and average age of target audience for a brand stands accepted.**

Informants of the study were asked to identify that the presence of popular celebrities just enhance the feel good factor for the consumers. The question was put to both the male and female respondents of the survey. A chi square test was performed based on the data obtained to find out if significant differences existed between the genders of respondents and their opinion that celebrities just enhances the feel good factor. The p-value obtained was 0.331 Since, $p>0.05$, **H8 which states that there is no significant difference between the gender of respondents and their opinion regarding popular celebrities enhancing the "feel good" factor for brands stands accepted.**

Limitations of the Study

- The study was conducted in the Kolkata market only. A pan-India study could have offered a better insight into the topic of study

- More variations in the profile of informants could have generated some more insightful findings

- The sample size was relatively small from which primary data has been collected. Hence the conclusions drawn are area specific and any generalization will need a cautious approach.

- The study was mainly based on the impact on brands. Inclusion of several other dimensions like the profitability of the company and others could have provided a different perspective to the study.

Conclusion

In a country like India, celebrities act as major opinion leaders and since awareness level is not the same for each and every individual, celebrities play a major role in brand recall. Celebrity endorsement decisively gives more visibility to the product endorsed. What-so ever the ground realities may be, but the masses still try to imbibe a style imitating the celebrities. Celebrities are helpful in initiating a desired state need among people. But celebrity endorsement is fraught with several dangers like overexposure, overshadowing the brand, negative publicity of the endorser to name a few. The Brands, taking into consideration all the related factors, can make best use of either the 'Bollywood stars' or 'Sports star' to endorse their product.

People prefer to watch their favorite personalities in various forms of endorsement for the products that they use. They always try to match up things of their use with that of their favorite stars whether of an actor or that of a sportsperson. Plethora of endorsements by different celebrities has not only positively impacted the Indian customers but has also influenced the purchase decision of the customers. In addition to this, the endorsements by popular celebrities brings quicker awareness of brands to the people and at the same time helps in building a positive image of the company or the brand. Even the newcomers in the field of sports and movies are appreciated in the form they come up in advertisements whether it is for the entire mass or for any particular region. The use of celebrity endorsements by various companies not only helps to create an image in the minds of people but also helps the firms to form a better acceptability and a better brand recall.

References

- Agrawal Pradeep and Dubey S.K (2012), "Celebrities: The Linking Pin between Brands and Their Customer", International Journal of Management and Business Studies; 2 (1), pp 56-60

- Sonwalkar Jayant, Kapse Manohar and Pathak Anuradha (2011), "Celebrity Impact- A Model of Celebrity Endorsement", Journal of Marketing and Communication; 7(1), pp 34-40

- Patra Supriyo and Datta Saroj (2010), "Celebrity Endorsement in India–Emerging Trends and Challenges", Journal of Marketing and Communication; 5(3), pp 16-23

- Schlecht Christina (2003), "Celebrities' Impact on Branding", available at www.forbes.com

- Sindhu Bhavana (2011), "Is Celebrity Endorsement a Midas touch or a landline", Gurukul Business Review; Vol. 7, pp 81-86

DISSERTATION – II

ANALYZING THE IMPACT OF CELEBRITY ENDORSEMENTS: GOODS V/S SERVICES

By Rishav Surana under the guidance of Prof. Kisholoy Roy

Abstract

With celebrity endorsements becoming the norm of the day with almost all major brands opting for it, it is very important to measure the effectiveness of the celebrities and the impact they have across on potential customers across product categories. This helps marketers to effectively choose the celebrities, based on the responses and the opinions of the potential customers. The objective of this study is to gauge the relative impact of celebrities on the basis of a comparative analysis between goods and services offerings, with the help of various judging parameters such as persuasive power,brand recall factor, enhancing of perceived quality, brand association, brand awareness, brand loyalty amongst others.

Key Words: Celebrity endorsements, brand recall, perceived quality, brand association, brand awareness, brand loyalty

1.0 Introduction

"Celebrity is an omnipresent feature of society, blazing lasting impressions in the memories of all who cross its path."
- Kurzman et.al (2007)

Celebrities going beyond their usual trade and endorsing products has become a common phenomenon in today's age. More and more marketers are taking this path in spite of the huge costs and the risks involved in signing celebrities to promote their products. This is primarily because across the world, more so in India, celebrities enjoy cult status amongst their legions of fans and have an unprecedented influencing power. The people of the nation have often put their favourite movie or cricket star on a pedestal and provided them demi god status, a trend more conspicuous in India than in foreign shores. It is this very craze amongst the fans that marketers aim to harness and hence, sign celebrities as endorsers.

The billion strong Indian markets is not an easy market to tap because of the various levels of diversities existing in the market. Be it religion, culture, beliefs, languages, norms, values or various strata of economic divisions, the Indian market presents a picture of various demographic divisions. This leads to variances in the purchasing power, preferences, methods of decision making etc. which the marketers need to keep in mind before placing their product and promoting it.

Today, the aim of marketers in India is to increase the persuasive power as well the recall value of their promotions. Advertisers have used various means to influence the consumer buying behaviour. Among them, the most popular and successful one has been celebrity endorsements.

The command and influence that celebrity endorsers enjoy over the masses has been higher than ever. It has been found time and again that, celebrity endorsements, if conceptualised and implemented in an appropriate manner, can provide the brand a competitive advantage and help build the brand equity. Research has depicted that celebrities make a subtle yet decisive impact on the everyday behaviour and decision making of individuals, as they form an illusionary interpersonal relationship with their idols. The preference for celebrity endorsements seems to have reached a crescendo and today, they have become an indispensible aspect of integrated marketing communication strategies. With the advancements in technologies and emergence of numerous new channels of communications, the companies can reach a larger base of customers in a more effective way and there is a greater scope of interactions between them. All of this has only enhanced the net impact celebrities have on the sales and brand image of products

In today's age of immense competition to grab the customer's attention and in turn, the market share, companies have more often than not resorted to the means of celebrity endorsements, be it for goods or for services.

This has allowed companies to engage with the potential customers at a greater level as they can easily connect with their celebrity role models and hence can relate to the products offered and bestow upon them their trust.

An innovative and effective use of celebrity to promote their product can help the company break the clutter, and make their products more visible among the scores of other companies having similar offerings

It is because of this proven effectiveness, that we are witnessing an unprecedented shift towards celebrity endorsements from that of traditional advertising focussed on print and television campaign. As celebrity endorsements are getting more popular, new concepts of celebrity licensing and celebrity partnerships have emerged, which involve greater involvement of celebrity with the brand.

Today, one can see celebrities endorsing products across categories, be it goods or services. Some of the advertisements featuring celebrities have acquired cult status, and are recalled even after years of it going off air.

With the emergence of new stars from various sporting disciplines such as badminton, chess, Formula 1, Tennis, wrestling and boxing etc., marketers have moved beyond the traditionally popular sectors of Bollywood and Cricket when choosing celebrities for products, although celebrities from these two fields still enjoy the maximum popularity amongst marketers.

As the Indian market is venturing into new avenues consistently, the product portfolio across goods and services is only expanding, and the demand for celebrity endorsements is only increasing. The services sector is also catching up with the traditionally celebrity dependent goods sector when it comes to celebrity endorsements. Gauging the mood of the marketers and the customers, one can say that the craze for celebrity endorsements is here to stay.

2.0 Literature Review

Celebrity endorsements in case of luxury branding have been found to have a negative impact on the brand (Park and Yi-Cheon, 2013). The results drawn on the basis of consumer responses suggest the ineffectiveness of the use of celebrities in the ads for luxury brands. This is primarily because it has been found that celebrities overshadow the luxury brand they endorse.

A moderate mismatch or incongruity between the image of the product and the image of the celebrity endorsing it (Lee andThorson, 2008) has been found to have a positive impact and on the basis of research it has been found out that it would produce more favourable responses in terms of influencing the purchase intentions of customers than in the case of either a complete match or extreme mismatch. The effects of such variations are even more pronounced in case of participants having high product involvement as compared to those with lower product involvement.

Celebrity endorsements, although a great tool for building a brand and its popularity, can have negative results (Patel, 2009) and may boomerang if not utilised properly by the company. This is because even celebrities have human shortcomings, and can fail in their field or get embroiled in controversies. This can in turn, have a negative impact on the product they endorse which might fail inspite of being of competitive quality. Some of the pros of having a celebrity are product gets quick attention, connection with the masses, brand differentiation and also builds the brand value as well as lends credibility. Some of the cons include the product getting overshadowed, becoming overtly dependent on the celebrity, or might lead to a clutter as a celebrity endorses multiple products.

In this globalised world, celebrity endorsements have become a rage worldwide as well as in India (Patra andDatta, 2010). The emergence of IMC has only added new dimensions. As advertisements become more elaborate and competitions increase, it has become very crucial to choose the right celebrity. The various methods for the same include 'Q' Rating Score, Principle of Congruity and other criteria such as familiarity of the celebrity, popularity and the FRED principle (Familiarity, Relevance, Esteem and Differentiation)

Today, due to increased competition, companies invest huge sums in advertisements, with an increased reliance on celebrity endorsements. The major reason behind this is that celebrities help in enhancing the brand recall as they bring better memorability for the brand and a better connect with the customer

(Dhotre and Bhol, 2010). It has been found that maximum recall is enjoyed in traditional entertainment channels and male celebrities are able to command a greater recall as compared to their female counterparts. In case of general brands, Film stars enjoy greater recall as compared to cricketers.

Another trend in the world of celebrity promotions is that of celebrity licensing, where the products are conjoined to the personal styles of the celebrities and involve their greater involvement as compared to celebrity endorsements, where the celebrity only appears in the advertisements. It has been found that consumers have a different outlook and attitude towards products endorsed by celebrity as compared to the products the celebrity is involved in the creation of. (Kapoor, 2013)

Various methods have been utilised to assess the effectiveness of a celebrity used to promote a brand. A new recall concept termed as celebrity aided brand recall and brand aided celebrity recall (Gnanapragash and Sekar, 2013) has been employed in order to identify selected celebrity aided recalls of the brand and certain brand aided recalls of the celebrity. The first celebrity that comes to mind when a brand is named (in spite of multiple celebrities endorsing it) is considered to be the best fit for the brand and this analysis helps the marketers in choosing the right celebrity. In case of celebrity aided brand recall, it was found that higher recalling was observed in case of congruency fit between the brand and celebrity.

Celebrity endorsements for products have a positive impact on the consumer buying behaviour. With the implementation of adaptive conjoint analysis and genetic algorithms in the advertising process, advertisers have newly approached the matching of product and celebrity attributes. (Zwillin and Fruchter, 2013).

3.0 Research Objective
- To study whether celebrities are more effective as endorsers of goods than services
- To study the significant difference between genders of respondents and their perceptions of relative effectiveness of endorsers of goods vis-a-vis services
- To study the impact of celebrities in enhancing the brand equity component of products, Goods v/s Services
- To study whether celebrities are more persuasive and have a higher recall factor as endorsers of goods or services
- To study whether celebrity endorsers enhance the perceived quality of goods more than that of services.
- To study the effectiveness of celebrities as endorsers of premium products, goods v/s services.

4.0 Research Hypotheses
H1:Celebrities areless effective as endorsers of goods than services.
H2: There is significant difference between genders of respondents and their perceptions of relative effectiveness of endorser of goods vis-a-vis services.
H3: Celebrities areless effective in enhancing the brand equity components of goods than services.

5.0 Research Methodology
55 individuals in the age bracket of 21-35 years were surveyed. Majority of the respondents were

students pursuing various courses in B-Schools while the rest were service holders or professionals. A combination of judgemental andconvenience sampling had been used for the research. A structured questionnaireconstructed using Likert scale was used to collect responses.

One sample T Test and Chi Square Test were conducted on the responses obtained.

Reliability Analysis of the questionnaire was conducted and the corresponding Cronbach's Alpha was found to be 0.803

6.0 Research Findings
6.1 Demographic Profile of Respondents-Graphical Representation

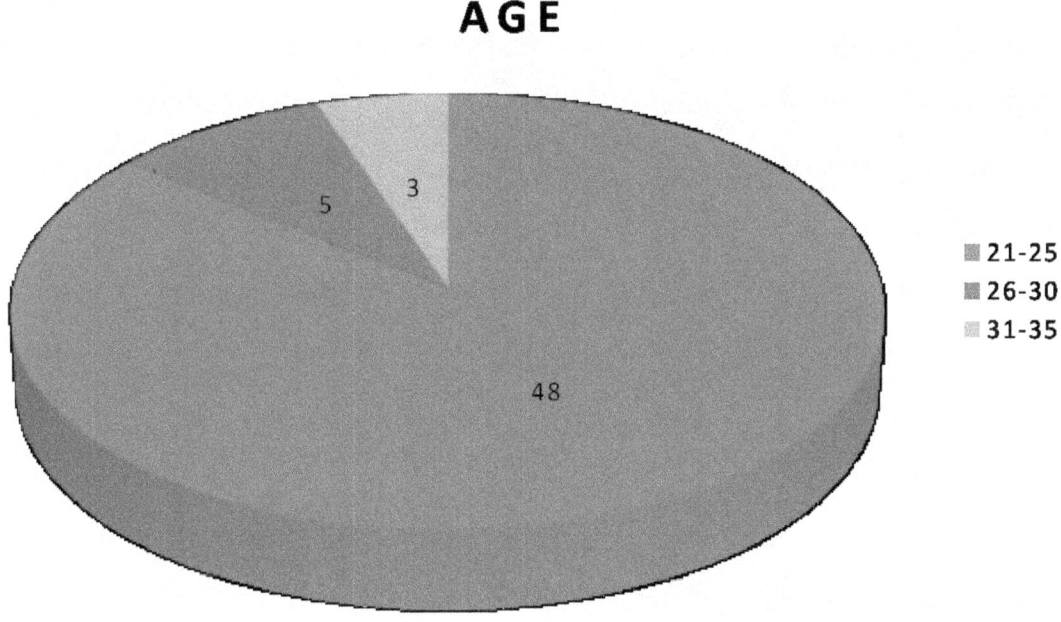

PROFESSION

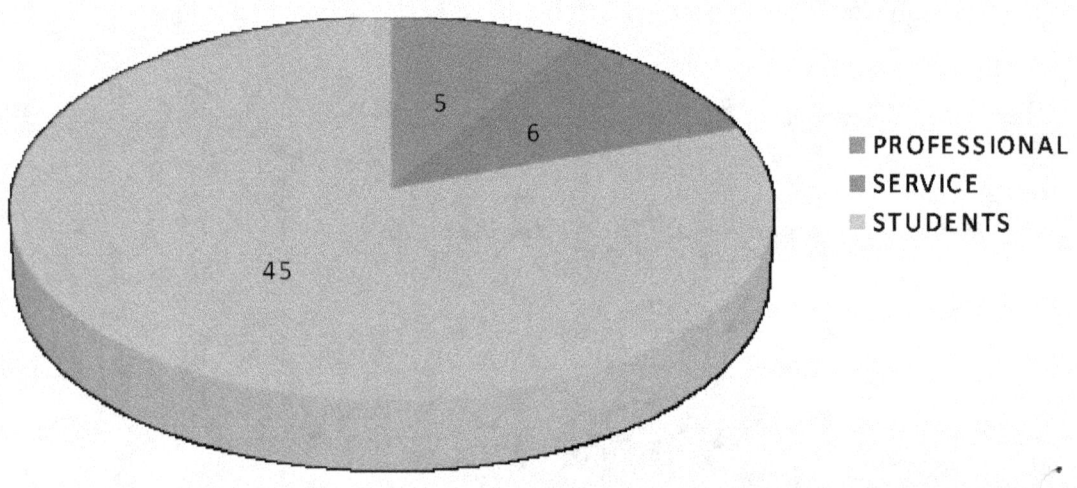

6.2 Testing of Hypotheses

H1: Celebrities are less effective as endorsers of goods than services.

H1$_a$: Celebrities are more effective as endorsers of goods than services.

H1: $\mu > 3$

H1$_a$: $\mu \leq 3$

A one sample t-test was employed to find out whether celebrities are more effective as endorsers of goods than services. p-value obtained was 0.001 (**Table 1**). There was a statistically significant difference between means ($p < .05$) and, therefore, we reject the null hypothesis **H1**which states that **Celebrities are less effective as endorsers of goods than services**and accept the alternate hypothesis **H1$_a$**which states **that Celebrities are more effective as endorsers of goods than services.**

TABLE 1

Mean	t value	p value	Standard error
10.4727	23.844	**0.001**	.31340

H2: There is significant difference between genders of respondents and their perceptions of relative effectiveness of endorsers of goods vis-avis services.

H2$_a$: There is no significant difference between genders of respondents and their perceptions of relative effectiveness of endorsers of goods vis-a-vis services.

A Chi Square test was conducted for testing H2.
The value of p obtained was 0.648. As the obtained value of p is greater than 0.05 (p>0.05), we accept the null hypothesis **H2**, which states that **There is significant difference between genders of respondents and their perceptions of relative effectiveness of endorser of goods vis-a-vis services.**

TABLE 2

	Value	Df	Asymp. Sig. (2-sided)
Pearson Chi-Square	2.479^a	4	.648
Likelihood Ratio	2.743	4	.602
Linear-by-Linear Association	.686	1	.408
N of Valid Cases	55		

H3: Celebrities are less effective in enhancing the brand equity components of goods than services.
H3$_a$: Celebrities are more effective in enhancing the brand equity components of goods than services.
H3: $\mu > 3$
H3$_a$: $\mu \leq 3$
A one sample t-test was employed to find out whether celebrities are more effective in enhancing the brand equity components of goods than services. p-value obtained was 0.001 (**Table 3**). There was a statistically significant difference between means ($p < .05$) and therefore, we can reject the null hypothesis **H3**which states that **Celebrities are less effective in enhancing the brand equity components of goods than services**and accept the alternate hypothesis **H3$_a$**which states **Celebrities are more effective in enhancing the brand equity components of goods than services.**

TABLE 3

Mean	t value	p value	Standard error
14.2364	32.012	**0.001**	.35101

7.0   Implications of the Study

It was found that celebrity endorsements are crucial for both goods as well as services but more crucial in case of goods. It was also highlighted that celebrities are more suitable and find greater acceptability for endorsing of goods as compared to that of services. The study revealed that celebrities have a greater persuasive power when they endorse goods as compared to services and celebrity endorsements in case of goods have a greater top of the mind retention in case of customers as compared to that of services. Results also show that Movie stars are more popular as endorsers both in the case of goods as well as services as compared to sport stars.

Results show that respondents can easily relate with celebrities associated with premium goods as they hold them in high regard.It was also found that celebrities enhance the perceived quality and contribute to the brand equity components more in case of goods than that of services while endorsing them. Hence, it can be concluded that celebrities have been found to have a greater impact on the potential customers in case of goods as compared to services.

8.0 Limitations of the Study

- Majority of the respondents were from the Kolkata area. Respondents from various parts of the country would have helped in getting a more Pan Indian view to the dissertation topic.
- The age profile of the respondents was highly skewed to the 21-25 age brackets. A greater representation of the various age profiles would have helped in obtaining a more holistic view, and in turn, led to a better understanding of the topic.
- The Gender distribution of the respondents was unequal, with the majority of respondents being male. An equal number of male and female respondents would have helped in obtaining an unbiased and more appropriate outcome of the research.
- Majority of the respondents were students. More number of respondents from other occupations would have helped in getting a complete picture of the customer preferences.

9.0 Conclusion

Celebrity Endorsement has become the buzzword amongst the marketers. In spite of the high costs of having a celebrity promoting ones brand and the various risks involved, they still opt for it as celebrities have a proven ability to influence the buying behaviour of the customer. The impact of celebrity endorsement is more pronounced in India as celebrities enjoy demi god status, and their vast legions of followers often blindly ape them in a quest to identify themselves on the same page as their celebrity idols. Many celebrity endorsers have helped to win back the credibility and customer confidence for companies in the time of crisis. Examples of chocolates and carbonated soft drinks company going for celebrity advocacy in the time of crisis and allegations further highlight the confidence that companies bestow upon celebrity endorsers.

Today, celebrity endorsement is used across market segments and across product categories, in goods as well as services. Celebrity endorsements in case of goods have existed much before celebrity endorsements for services caught up. Respondents believe that celebrities endorsing goods have a larger impact on the customers than as endorsers of services.

Moreover, a look in to the Indian advertisement industry shows that celebrity endorsements in the case of goods are more widespread, both in terms of sub categories of goods and the number of competitors.

References

- ZwillingMoti, Fruchter Gila (2013), "Matching Product AttributesTo Celebrities Who Reinforce the Brand", *Journal of Advertising Research*, 53(4) pp. 391-410

- Gnanapragash T Joel and PC Sekar (2013), "Celebrity-Aided Brand Recall and Brand-Aided

Celebrity Recall: An Assessment of Celebrity Influence Using the Hierarchy of Effects Model", *The IUP Journal of Brand Management*, 10(3), pp. 47-67

- KapoorPayal S. (2013), "Exploring Celebrity Licensing asOpposed to Celebrity Endorsement : A Consumer Perspective", *Journal of Marketing and Communication*, 9(1), pp. 13-19

- PatraSupriyo, DattaSaroj Kumar (2012), "Celebrity Selection & Role of Celebritiesin creating Brand Awareness and Brand Preference - A Literature Review", *Journal of Marketing and Communication*,8(2) , pp. 48-57

- DhotreMeenal P, BholaSarang S (2010), "Analytical Study of Association Between Celebrity Advertising and Brand Recall", *The IUP Journal of Brand Management*, 7(1/2), pp. 25-50.

- Patel Pratik C (2009), "Impact of Celebrity Endorsement on Brand Acceptance", *TheICFAI University Journal of Consumer Behavior*, 4(1), pp. 36-45.

- Lee Jung Gyo, Thorson Esther (2008), "The Impact of Celebrity-Product Incongruence on the Effectiveness of Product Endorsement", *Journal of Advertising Research*, September 2008, 48(3), pp. 433-449.

- Park Young Sun, Yi-CheonYim Mark (2013), "Too Much Spotlight: The Role Of Celebrities In Luxury Brand Advertising", *American Academy of Advertising Conference Proceedings*, pp. 165-165.

about the author

Prof. Kisholoy Roy is an Accredited Management Teacher certified by AIMA, New Delhi. He has several publications including books, articles, case studies and research papers in the domain of marketing management. Roy is a competent and popular faculty in the above said discipline and he has manifold creative interests apart from pursuing management literature.

www.ingramcontent.com/pod-product-compliance
Lightning Source LLC
Chambersburg PA
CBHW081859170526
45167CB00007B/3077